"I wish this book had been available in 1995! When I became a veterinarian that year, I also entered the world of sales. I have read various books on 'how to sell' and have even attended numerous sales training workshops, but *Selling By Serving* provides a masterful insight regarding what it truly means to sell. The author not only details a practical approach to the art of selling but he does so through a servant's heart, something that is often missed when sales becomes 'just about the numbers.' I encourage everyone in sales to read this book and apply what it truly means to sell by serving."

 —***Lance V. Fox, DVM,*** *V.P. at Archer Daniels*
 Midland and author of "No Place But UP!"

"Clancy beautifully highlights that at the root of every successful sale is the idea that the sales rep serves the customer, not sales quotas. That is the core value quality of successful salespeople in any industry and it's where other sales books miss the mark. Clancy provides a refreshing and meaningful take on this integral theme through metaphorical and intelligent insights."

 —***Chris Lansing,*** *top performer from door-to-door*
 sales to software employed by NASA

"*Selling By Serving* is such a delight to read! Clancy has avoided the typical sales training 'do-this-and-do-that-and-you-will-get-this-result' kind of a book. Instead, he has introduced the missing ingredient in many sales approaches, which is, 'How has my time benefited the client?' I spent 40-plus years coaching salespeople and agree that when you practice the art of servanthood you will watch your results soar. His results speak to the usefulness of this material. This book should be in every salesperson's library."

> —**Fred Martsolf,** *Sales Manager at Cargill Animal Nutrition and Purina Animal Nutrition*

"Clancy provides a vital link between the sales process and what is most important—the true art of relationship building. His ability to weave stories of substance into the narrative is second-to-none. I highly recommend this book to anyone who is looking for, or wishes to reinforce, that missing component in one's definition of sales success!"

> —**Mike St. John,** *Professional Consultant to Entrepreneurs & Small Businesses*

SELLING BY SERVING

Find Fulfillment in Your Career and Sell
More Than You Ever Thought Possible

―― ℃℧ ――

CLANCY CLARK

Publishing consultant: David Wogahn, AuthorImprints.com

CONTENTS

ACKNOWLEDGEMENTS

To my beloved Devon, the woman who supports me in everything I do. Thank you for inspiring me to always be moving my own happiness and fulfillment to the next level.

To Scott Forbes, for helping with the words to make my stories and ideas come alive. You are a clever craftsman and a good friend.

To the gang at Philosophy Communication, for so beautifully bringing my platform together under one terrific brand. Thanks for every memorable step we've taken together.

To the animals I've had the privilege of raising and training, for whom I've cared and with whom I've worked. I have witnessed the miracle of welcoming you into this world, and I have been by your side as you've departed it. Thank you for all you have taught me, and for that which you continue to teach me. You have enriched my life beyond my power to convey.

To the farmers and ranchers whom I've had the honor of serving. I am in awe of your tireless work to feed and clothe the world. Your dedication to the animals and the land, your family values, your honesty, and your ethics are timeless. Thank you for letting me be a part of your success.

To my Dad, who shared with me his love for the outdoors. Thank you so much for my J.C. Penney backpack and for taking me on my first backpacking trip to Glacier National Park. You planted a seed that continues to grow and flourish, one that nourishes my spirit every time I immerse myself in nature.

A NOTE FROM THE AUTHOR

Making a sale is never a cause; it's a result.

This book is not centered around how to sell more products or services. There are plenty of those kinds of books out there; they generally present some set of steps for you to learn and apply so you can "sell your widgets to anyone" and/or "leave your competition in the dust." While following a particular method may allow you to enjoy a measure of success—such as sales commissions, awards, or nice vacation trips—meeting any of those measures really only takes you halfway to the success you could achieve.

If you want to truly feel success, if you want to fully and deeply understand what it means to be successful, you have to do more than follow a set of steps. You have to go beyond any particular method.

I know. I've done it. For that reason, I believe I can help you find success in your sales career that far exceeds any quantifiable standards.

In my 30-plus years of successful sales experience, I have quickly risen to the top of three different agri-business companies, in three different decades, in three very different geographical regions of the United States. In each case I have started from a base of zero sales and had to learn the technical side of what I was selling in short order. In each case I have built my book of business in down markets for the industries into which I sold. Those are measurable results that have drawn a seemingly endless parade of sales managers and fellow sales professionals to approach me at company conferences and awards banquets and ask, "How did you do what you've done?"

My response has always been some form of the following: "I can't tell you exactly how, because, to me, there's no method, no step-by-step, A-B-C way to make a sale." Sure, I acknowledge that there are some steps that are common to every selling relationship, which I'll cover early in the book. But following these steps alone will never be enough to bring true fulfillment in sales.

Another thing I've run across during my career is far too many sales professionals wondering why they're not fulfilled in their careers even though they're "hitting their numbers." I have also seen a high rate of failure among people new to sales who seem lost or overwhelmed trying to "learn how to sell." Then there is the surprisingly high number of seasoned sales professionals who are in a rut; even though they may be making very good money, they're asking themselves, "Is this all there is?"

Contrasting these encounters with the everyday fulfillment and success I've had in sales has made me want to reach out and help these people. The values and principles by which I've conducted myself during my sales career are, I truly believe, what have helped me find so much satisfaction and fulfillment in my professional and personal life. Letting more people know about these values and principles is the reason I wrote this book.

Sales is the most human of careers. Sales is about relationships. By immersing yourself in truly developing each relationship, you will enjoy the profession to its fullest. You will find fulfillment, happiness, and financial success beyond anything you may have previously thought possible.

I firmly believe that only by placing something other than "selling more widgets" or "leaving the competition in the dust" as the highest priority can a salesperson feel fulfilled and truly happy in his or her work. The beautiful irony here is that, if you are fulfilled in your sales career, if you bring that fulfillment to everything you do—rather than trying to extract success from it—you will sell much more than if you pursue sales numbers as an end unto itself.

Such a mentality has certainly been true for me. And I believe it can be for you.

Many of the stories and examples in the book come from experiences that are part of living the life I have imagined, the life I have always set out to live, the life I continue to enjoy. It is my sincere wish that you will find inspiration within these pages to achieve the kind of success I'm talking about and, therefore, realize for yourself the life you've always imagined.

That's what this book is about.

INTRODUCTION

The Road That Has Brought Me Here...

A vocation is not a destination. It's not a definition of a person, a singular way to describe exactly who that man or woman is. A vocation is something in which we engage to meet another purpose, perhaps many other purposes. A vocation isn't the totality of a person's life; it's a part, likely an important part, of that life. But it doesn't make up the whole of a human being.

There's so much more.

All my professional iterations have been interesting, but the journey through them has revealed what's most interesting to me...what the work has allowed me to do. The best thing about those jobs has not necessarily been the lifestyle my success has allowed me to enjoy. No, the best thing is how I feel about what I've done and how I've been able to do it.

What is it that I've done?

I have been "of service." I have been of service to the ranchers and farmers and dairy producers who are now, or who have been, my customers. I've also been of service to the people who these farmers and ranchers feed, and I've been of service to the people with whom these farmers and ranchers do business, the people who sell them the supplies they need, the people who purchase the products they produce.

I've been of service to people close to me as well as many people I've never met.

I have probably never met you, but I would very much like to be of service to you, to help you in your own career and your own life, to help you reach the goals that you have and realize a fulfillment that you may never have thought possible.

Being of service is what gets me going, it's what makes me look forward to the workday ahead, and it's what makes me feel satisfied when the workday comes to an end. A career in sales is not, I believe, an end in itself but a part of my personal vision I have for myself.

I didn't start my sales career with the goal of being of service to other people; I started out anxious to make sales, earn money, meet and surpass goals. Burdened by those insular motivations, I was not quite as successful as I wanted to be. Only when I realized the true fulfillment that came with being of service did I start to reach sales goals, to hit numbers, and to exceed what I'd done the year before.

That's not to say there haven't been times in my career when I've lost focus, when I've chased the "pot of gold" instead of serving my customers first and foremost. The result, without exception, was that material success began to slip away and the sales business felt like a struggle, a strain. The irony here is that when I started to look at myself and my career in a much more objective fashion, I realized that concentrating on my quotas and what's in it for me got in the way of my achieving quotas and getting everything I could out of the endeavor.

My first goal with this book is to help you avoid this mindset, which traps so many sales professionals. My second goal is to help you find the kind of fulfillment and satisfaction I have found in my sales career and my life.

Just another day at the office with one of my "co-workers"

PART ONE

BEFORE YOU GO
BEYOND THE METHOD

CHAPTER 1

PURSUING SALES MASTERY

"Find something you love, and go after it, with all your heart."—Motivational speaker Jim Abbott, who was born with one arm, yet pitched in the major leagues for ten years

When I think back to the road I've taken, the road that has brought me here to the life I love in Southern Colorado, I consider the many experiences that have shaped me into the person I am today. My decisions haven't always been good—I'm human; I've made mistakes—but, on balance, I've been able to reach many of my goals, goals that I set for myself many years ago when I began my career in sales living in Montana.

I started to realize those goals when I changed the way I looked at myself, both as a salesman and as a person. Instead of simply being a representative of a company—someone whose job it is to move product on behalf of my employer—I began to think of myself as something much more: a partner, a guide, a leader, a problem solver. I thought of myself as a person who could bring something more to the relationship between buyer and seller.

What I started to bring to the job was a servant's heart.

Different people have different definitions of exactly what a servant's heart is, so it would probably be beneficial for me to explain what the term means to me. A person who brings a servant's heart to a task is someone who puts the task ahead of him or herself, ahead of his or her aspirations, and ahead of any personal considerations. Bringing a servant's heart to the job of sales means concentrating 100% on the customer's needs and wants, guiding the customer, and looking out for the customer's best interests. If you're selling with a servant's heart, you're simply matching the customer's needs with something you have to offer that can solve the customer's problem. You are not selling for any other reason.

A servant's heart is all too often the missing element in the business of sales today. So much literature about the subject of sales, all the instruction about becoming a better salesperson, starts with a method, takes you through that method, and ends with a quick review of what you are likely to achieve by following the method. Like a recipe.

Learning and following a recipe can make you an excellent cook in much the same way learning and following a method can make you a successful salesperson. You can follow recipes developed by someone else and serve delicious meals just as you can follow another person's sales method and meet your numbers and earn commissions and bring home a handsome income.

For some people that's satisfaction enough.

But it never was for me.

Before I started my career in sales, I was a young man raising working dogs in Montana. These dogs—primarily Border Collies and Australian Shepherds—amazed me the way they could be trained to move and control herds of sheep. I wanted to learn how to train them the best I possibly could. I needed guidance, however, and I needed proper training myself as I was worried that I might learn a poor or ineffective way of training these special dogs. The fact was that I was terrified at the prospect of ruining young pups for the chore, the chore that they were born to perform.

I shared my worries with fellow dog trainers in attendance at a presentation put on by the world-renowned Jack Knox. Much to my surprise, pretty much all of the other trainers shared my fears and believed that what we were about to learn—Jack Knox's tried-and-true dog-training method—would help us overcome our trepidation.

A Scotsman, Jack was gruff and assertive. He asked the assembled crowd: "Whose dog would like to be put through the paces?" One person after another brought his or her dog to the front, where Jack drilled them each for many intense minutes. Every dog under Jack's guidance heard the same commands, reacted the same way, and performed effectively with almost military precision. It was a very impressive demonstration.

Jack's reputation for training and producing some of the world's best working dogs was spotless, and he put it on display right before me. I borrowed his structured approach in the ensuing years and had terrific success training dogs. I liked to say that Jack's method kept me "between the ditches" when it came to training dogs, and any worries about ruining them washed away as I mimicked everything Jack had taught us at the clinic.

A few years later, I put 1,000 miles on my truck specifically for the purpose of attending a clinic hosted by Glyn Jones in the Canadian province of Alberta. Considered the guru of Border Collie training, this Welshman had won multiple International Sheepdog Trials and was considered to be the best credentialed trainer in the world. Glyn was cheerful and fun-loving, as happy to be around dogs and other people as a man could possibly be. His broad smile and upbeat nature kept the mood light as he commenced his clinic by asking for someone to bring him a dog.

The first dog, a large male, was presented to Glyn by its owner. But the dog was in no mood to follow any orders. The dog pulled so hard on his leash that he was choking himself, so excited was he to get to the herd. "He's a little rough with the sheep," said the owner apologetically.

"Right, then," responded Glyn as if he hadn't heard the owner. "Let's let him have a go."

With that the owner unhooked the leash and what happened next can only be described as complete pandemonium. The dog exploded toward the sheep, the sheep scattered in all directions, the noise was deafening. I watched the scene for a moment and thoughts of a Road Runner cartoon flashed through my head.

Then I turned my attention to Glyn, expecting him to take hold of the situation, to magically calm the dog and, in turn, the sheep, and to reveal his own proprietary method. Glyn's method had, of course, made him world-famous, and I eagerly awaited the presentation that this magical dog-training genius had used to earn such stature. Surely, he'd have a command or a motion or a look that would bring some order to the chaos that was going on behind him.

But he didn't. He didn't even seem to care.

Glyn turned his back on the action and began to tell us all a story. It was a funny tale about how he was walking his Border Collie back home when he ran into a friend who was walking his own dog of the same breed. Glyn and his friend decided to step into a local pub for a couple of pints, and they tied their dogs' leashes to a post outside. A few weeks later, Glyn started to notice that his dog, a female, had put on a little weight. Then a little more. All concentrated around the belly. Yes, his dog and his friend's dog had gotten quite frisky with each other during the short time Glyn and his friend were enjoying their ales. The result was a litter of puppies, and Glyn would keep one of them. Not surprisingly, the dog turned out to be another one of Glyn's champion Border Collies.

My recollection of hearing the story was bittersweet because I couldn't truly appreciate it; I was too busy wondering if this legendary dog trainer was crazy or maybe even a con artist. Had I really registered, paid a significant fee, and driven 1,000 miles to see this fiasco?

I kept feeling my emotions change from confusion to rage to wonderment at the whole spectacle as the madness continued between the large male dog and the frantic sheep. Glyn kept on with his stories, occasionally looking over his shoulder at the dog's handiwork. At one point a sheep came running past us, causing Glyn to happily snap, "Hoy dog." My jaw dropped in disbelief when that happened because "hoy dog" is not a formal sheepdog command of any kind. I'd never heard the comment before in my life. Was Glyn playing with a full deck? I was seriously regretting that I'd made the effort to attend this farce and considered standing up, turning away, and commencing my long drive home riddled with disappointment.

Then it happened! The dog ran out of gas. He plopped down right behind Glyn. Relieved, the sheep stopped too. Glyn looked over his shoulder, turned back to us, and revealed a new facial expression... one that suggested his serious side. He stopped what he was saying in mid-sentence, turned to the dog, and said, quietly but firmly, "Now get back." The dog responded positively right away. In fact, from that moment on, the dog was the most competent dog I'd ever seen. "Bring 'em, Laddie...steady there," said Glyn to the dog. Glyn started walking out to the field as the dog dropped his head and brought the pack of sheep with him like a champ. For the next few minutes, Glyn put the dog through his paces, and the dog's reaction to each and every command was stellar. "That'll do, Laddie," said Glyn when the drills were done. The dog came away from the sheep and walked right up to Glyn, who gently clipped the leash onto the dog's collar, gave the dog back over to his owner, turned to the rest of us, and calmly said: "Right, then, let's have another dog out here."

I was in shock. My jaw dropped, and my eyes were as big as saucers. Had I not been there to see it myself, I wouldn't have believed it was possible. I realized at that moment that I'd just witnessed something I'd never seen before. I'd witnessed mastery.

Over the next two days, I talked to Glyn often and watched him very closely. I listened to everything he said and paid attention to everything he did around the dogs. To my amazement, what he did when dealing with one dog was often completely different than the way he would deal with another dog. I wondered why that was—what was the pattern I was missing? What steps was he following? What was his method? I kept watching Glyn more intently as he gave very little instruction on techniques or mechanics associated with dog training. He simply demonstrated the skills and instincts he'd learned through his decades of experience. He worked on a level that transcended any method. There was no "Step #1, Step #2, Step #3..." to his work because—as he rightly pointed out—every dog is unique.

"So true," I said to myself as I started to appreciate that Glyn wasn't teaching us any single method that would help us turn young pups into effective and capable working dogs. Glyn was training us, the trainers! He was showing us that training a dog is only 20 to 25 percent about following a particular method. The remaining 75 to 80 percent of training is about instincts, about learning and getting to know your own instincts as well as those of a particular dog, and developing a relationship that allows the two of you to work together so that you're almost thinking the same thoughts simultaneously. Every relationship between a trainer and a dog is different. A dog knows this. A person needs to learn it. Only when the trainer appreciates the unique nature of his or her interaction with each dog, only when the trainer goes *Beyond The Method*, can both the trainer and dog work toward achieving mastery.

It was on that field in Alberta that I started to realize something I never knew I had in me. I had instincts; I had an innate understanding of the dogs and of each dog's unique quirks and capabilities. I had within me the tools I needed to work toward achieving mastery.

When I got back to Montana, I brought with me an entirely new outlook on dog training. Prior to the trip I had always enjoyed working with Border Collies, knowing how a dog derives so much of his or her quality of life through service. Whether they're performing specialized tasks or simply hanging around the house as the family pet, dogs live to serve their owners. Being of service to their owners translates for so many dogs into realizing their quality of life.

Applying what I learned about myself, thanks to Glyn, made me fall in love with the work and understand that I wanted to serve any dog I was training at the same level as (or an even higher level than) that dog was serving me. This new outlook elevated my self-confidence, and I could tell that I was practicing my skills on a much higher plane—to the point that I too would go on to train Border Collies who would become highly decorated champions themselves.

When I made the professional transition to a career in sales a few years later, I realized that the same mentality applied. I could have taken my company's sales training method and gotten results that were more than adequate, providing a handsome income and a comfortable lifestyle. That would have been fine and would have brought me a great deal of satisfaction.

With Griff, competing at a sheepdog trial in Alberta, Canada

But was that good enough? Would simply making sales and earning a good living be my picture of success? Moreover, is that good enough for you?

My background had taught me that a method could take me only so far. A method could provide me only with a scrap of the much larger roadmap I would need to have a successful and fulfilling career in sales. But if I brought a servant's heart to a sales career, if I invested in something more than meeting numbers and gaining commissions, if I realized that as a salesman I would be there to be of service to my customers, I could work toward attaining mastery in sales.

I wanted to reach my highest potential and achieve the kind of fulfillment that had filled my heart after meeting Glyn Jones and applying what I learned about myself—applying what was really special and unique about me—as a result. I knew that I had to do more than simply follow a method. I had to go *Beyond The Method* in the constant pursuit of mastery in the field of sales.

Nearly 30 years ago, I made the commitment that I don't work for money. I earn money; it's one of the rewards I receive for doing my job well. But I work for many other reasons, reasons that mean more to me than money ever could.

I want to help you do the same.

CHAPTER 2

THE SELLING CYCLE

What is selling if it's nothing more than separating other people from their money?

Many people will point at the commonly understood selling cycle, often depicted in a graphic, and announce that selling is all about "meeting, connecting, pitching, and closing the sale."

TRADITIONAL SELLING CYCLE

1. Prospect For Leads
2. Initiate Contact
3. Qualify The Lead
4. Present Offer
5. Overcome Objections
6. Close The Sale
7. Generate Referral

That's "The Method", that's the traditional way it's done, that's the way sales is done, has always been done, and that's the way sales will be done for the foreseeable future. It's as easy as that. That's "The Method" by which sales are made, right? Whether you're selling widgets or washing machines, that's how it's done. Right?

I believe there's something critically important missing in this logic.

As mentioned earlier, a simple method can get it done in sales. You can "follow the dots" and make sales. But are you getting the most out of your sales call? Every customer is different; every interaction is different. You're a human being. Your customers are human too. Every interaction is its own story, and every interaction allows you to do something unique in order to serve the person to whom you're trying to sell.

> You may call the person to whom you're selling a "client" or perhaps a "prospect" if that person has never bought from you before. Throughout this book I will identify any purchaser or potential purchaser as a "customer," unless I'm referring specifically to a prospect. "Customer" is a common word used to identify anyone who is on the buying side of the equation.

I didn't know or appreciate that sort of thinking when I started my career in sales. I thought there was indeed a simple method, a path that would lead anyone willing to tread upon it to sales success. But then I recalled my years training dogs and how my outlook on that endeavor changed after meeting Glyn Jones. A method is a roadmap. A method is a recipe. A method is the smallest portion of success in dog training; the big chunk of success is going beyond any method.

So, doesn't it make sense to go *Beyond The Method* in sales too?

The fact is, there is no method in sales that can take you as far as you can possibly go. There's no paint-by-numbers way of making a sale that will bring out the full potential of the relationship. If you keep following the same sort of method, you'll keep getting the same results. Think about the old piece of advice: "Keep doin' what you're doin' and you'll keep gettin' what you're getting.'" If you want to put something more into your sales pitch, you have a better chance to get something more out of it. You need to go *Beyond The Method*.

Recall my separate experiences with Jack Knox and Glyn Jones. Jack had a method that informed the way he trained each and every dog. Glyn had something more. Glyn brought standard dog-training disciplines with him, but he never saw two dogs that were exactly alike. Each one had unique needs and performed optimally when those unique needs were met by the trainer. While Jack displayed a method for dog training, Glyn didn't stop with any method. He analyzed each situation for itself and tailored his training to that situation. He displayed mastery.

Glyn Jones inspired me to go *Beyond The Method* in everything I do. I really took his message to heart when I got into the business of sales, taking pains to lead my customers instead of selling to them and to treat them all as the individuals they are.

But first allow me to make one concession. Before anyone can go *Beyond The Method* or achieve mastery in sales, there are some steps that a salesperson—every salesperson—must follow every time that salesperson gets ready for a call. These are steps that should be considered universal, steps that everyone in the business of sales needs to know and exercise. You don't just walk up to someone at random, tell that person you've got something to sell, and then expect that person to buy it from you. Conversely, no one approaches you and says, "I'll buy whatever you've got." There is important groundwork that needs to be cultivated if you intend to be successful in sales. I refer to this groundwork as "The Nuts and Bolts of Sales."

The things that every salesperson needs to do are centered around asking questions, reacting to them, and pivoting to the next subject. So, let's review a few of the questions and answers that are basic to the salesperson:

> *What is your job?*
> - It's to sell your products or services
> - It's to meet sales goals
> - It's to make money for your company and yourself

> *How do you sell your products and services?*
> - By telling prospects and customers that what you're selling will improve profitability
> - By lowering prices or offering a volume discount
> - By claiming that what you're selling will improve the life of an end user

Questions and answers like these reflect the philosophies that most salespeople learn and bring to the job. These questions and answers are with them at every sales call, every interaction with a customer. They could, however, change their mindset and put themselves in the pro-verbial shoes of the customer. Such a shift in perspective could open up all sorts of new avenues...

> *Have you ever thought about Needs-Satisfaction Selling?*
> - You should always understand the needs of your customer
> - You should always know how what you're selling satisfies those needs

- Fulfilling a need solves a problem for your customer—never forget that

When you start to ask yourself these questions—as well as others—you realize there's more to selling than just having some product or service at a price and offering it up. You also realize there's more than one way to answer the same question, depending on whether you're selling to a business or to an end user, whether you're selling to a mom-and-pop shop or to a huge international retailer, whether you're selling an item that needs to be consumed in short order like seafood or something that can stay on the shelves for weeks like canned beans.

Asking yourself the first two questions—"What is your job?" and "How do you sell?"—will not yield any kind of insight for you. Asking the third type of question, however, will start you on the road toward realizing that you, the salesperson, can indeed be of service to someone else.

Bringing a servant's heart and satisfying a need is what you must be doing as a salesperson in order to be of service to your customer. It's how you make yourself an asset to your customer's business or personal life. Seeing the need from the customer's perspective and beginning to understand what that person across the table is trying to achieve is so important. What is his or her motive? What is he or she trying to achieve by making a particular purchase? Asking questions like these and accepting the learnings that answers afford is the first key to successful selling.

Questions lead not just to answers, but also to more questions. If you start to ask questions, you should quickly realize that questions never can and never should end. There's always more to know. Be curious about your customer, about the person's needs and wants and perhaps even the customer's most strongly held desires, short-term and long-term. Does your customer wish to grow the business? Is he looking to sell the business in a few years? Would she like to turn the business over to a child or other family member in 20 years? You should know these things and more. Never let that curiosity be satisfied, because an incurious salesperson is a person who will settle for a method that he or she applies to every sales call.

> Many people in sales, and in other professions, have a subconscious belief that asking questions reveals a weakness. That mindset comes from a belief that says, "I'm the expert on what I'm selling, and, therefore, I must appear to have all the answers." Yes, you may be the expert on what you're selling, but are you the expert on what the person across from you is looking for?

Curiosity may have killed the proverbial cat, but it will only help you make your sales career in cat food as vibrant as it can possibly be.

CHAPTER 3

THE SEVEN STEPS OF SELLING BY SERVING

've said it before, and I'll say it again: Sales is not about "making a killing." It's not about meeting numbers, it's not about scoring a hefty commission, it's not about you!

Sales is about your customer. It's about helping your customer, being of service to that person, improving his or her situation.

Bring a servant's heart to every sales call, and you'll bring a lot more to your customer than any of your competitors can possibly bring.

But before you do that, remember that there are seven steps that are a part of every sales process. These steps don't represent a method of any kind on their own, but they are important to understand and recognize because they're universal to any selling situation.

No matter what you're selling, you need to observe these steps as you proceed with your customer, walking side by side down the path to purchase. Are you selling a big-ticket item like a house? If you are, you know instinctively that the buyer is very emotionally wrapped up in the purchasing decision, and it only makes sense to go through each of these steps rather deliberately.

Perhaps you're selling something that appears to require less introspection from a buyer, something like a lawn mower. Each of these steps still applies. After all, what you're selling is not just a lawnmower, a

hunk of metal with an engine and a blade. You're selling a tool that is absolutely a means to an end. That end could be a finely manicured yard for a person who spends summers fussing over every detail of a house's landscape. Lawn mowing could be an unwelcome weekly hassle for a homeowner who'd rather spend his summer afternoons on the lake or reading a book or driving kids to all their activities. Speaking of kids, the buyer could be buying the lawn mower because his kid is interested in earning a few dollars over the summer mowing lawns around the neighborhood.

Even if you're selling something as pedestrian as penny candy, you will go through the first six steps with a customer and, quite possibly, all seven—the last being objections. I know I have objections to any candy that's banana flavored.

Information that helps you help your customer is there for you to learn. You just have to be willing to ask questions.

Never forget that you're guiding, you're leading, you're helping the person across from you realize that what you have to offer is going to solve a problem or fulfill a need or allow that person to turn a lifelong dream like owning a home into a reality.

CHAPTER 4

PREPARATION

A lot of people in sales believe the sales call is the beginning of something—and it is. Hopefully, an initial sales call is the beginning of a long and fruitful relationship for both parties. But I think it's a lot more important to look at a sales call as the culmination of something that's all too often overlooked in our business: It's the culmination of a great deal of preparation.

Preparation should never end; it's a cyclical part of any salesperson's job. Recall what I noted earlier about pursuing mastery, it's waking up every morning with a mindset of learning something new. That mindset always has me being a student rather than a teacher, an important distinction.

Preparation is vitally important. It means knowing everything you can learn about a customer: likes and dislikes, the disposition of the business, the person's management style, whether or not there's some personality quirk that would be useful to know.

I've learned during my years in sales that few businesses are as devoted to preparation as a farm or a ranch is. Farmers, for instance, plan months ahead to determine when they're going to plant and harvest crops. Farmers and ranchers plan an entire season ahead when looking for buyers of their commodity at a certain price. They plan years ahead when considering crop rotation, for instance. They plan for contingencies like the weather, which never seems to work hand in hand with their best laid plans.

Preparation on a farm or a ranch never ends; someone, or some animal, is always preparing for what's next.

Perhaps the most interesting preparation I've seen during my sales career on farms and ranches is that put forth by dairy cows and the farmers who care for them. A dairy cow is expected to produce milk for 305 days in a row, and each of those days the cow is making a physical effort that is equivalent to a human being running a marathon. Every day!

> **"By failing to prepare, you are preparing to fail."**
> **—Benjamin Franklin**

So, what happens to the cow on the 306th day? That's when she starts her "dry" period—when the preparation really gets started. She prepares. The farmer who owns her prepares. The vet who treats her prepares. The dairy nutritionist—that's me, of course—prepares. We all prepare for the cow's next 305 days in succession when she must produce milk.

It works like this: In order for a cow to produce any milk at all, she must be lactating. In order to lactate, of course, she must have given birth to a calf. In order to give birth, she must...well, let's just say there's a 60-day "dry" period for every dairy cow, a two-month span of time during which she must:

- Rebuild her body condition
- Replenish mineral stores in her liver
- Complete the gestation of an unborn calf

The dry period for a cow—and the first 24 hours of her calf's life—are vital to the health of the cow and to the health of any dairy farm's business. In addition to providing proper nutrition during the dry period, the farmer and his team must also provide vaccinations, eliminate internal and external parasites, and manage the health of the cow's udders. These 60 days are all about preparation for the job every dairy cow must perform.

Once the calf is successfully born at the end of the 60 days, the dairy cow—who's just given birth—will, of course, start to lactate. Only then is she able to produce milk, and she'll do it for the next 305 days. That period of time is when all the preparation comes into play. Only a healthy cow, a cow who's been cared for during her dry period, can produce a proper quantity of fresh, wholesome milk every day for that long. She must be fully prepared to handle the challenge.

Few salespeople have 60 days to prepare for a sales call. Of course, few salespeople run the equivalent of a marathon every day for the rest of the year either. But just because working in sales is not as physically demanding doesn't mean you don't have to be prepared.

When I'm preparing to call on my dairy farm customers, I go through a checklist of five important things I need to address:

1. Appearance
2. Prospect Knowledge
3. Intended Outcome
4. Supporting Materials
5. Mental State

The first is appearance—how do I look? It's important that I look the part of a dairy nutrition expert. If I were to show up in a Giorgio Armani suit, an Hermès tie, and a pair of Salvatore Ferragamo loafers, I'd be laughed out of the county. I'd also do a number on those shoes and the rest of the outfit when I got knee-deep in the cow pen doing my investigating as it pertains to the cows' nutrition and health.

Prospect knowledge is another aspect of preparation that calls on you to ask questions. Ask questions of people who may know that prospect, learn everything you can about the prospect, find out where your interests intersect, subjects you should avoid—you should even learn if your prospect has an annual vacation that takes him or her away from business at a certain time every year. Yes, even learning something that seemingly unimportant can be the difference between a sale and "getting the gate," which is farm sales slang for being told not to let the door hit you in the hindquarters on your way out.

As your sales call approaches, come to a decision about your intended outcome. Is this a meeting with a longtime client, one who always buys from you this time of year? Unless that client's circumstances have changed dramatically, your intended outcome is to make a sale that's similar to the sale you made a year ago at this time. Are you meeting a prospect for the first time? Then your intended outcome would be more like being asked to leave samples or maybe a list of references. No matter what your expectations are regarding a sales call, you need to bring your idea of the intended outcome with you. Only by doing so can you gauge if you're making progress or if you're simply "spinning your wheels," if you're wasting your time, and, more important, if you're wasting your prospect's time.

Knowing what supporting materials to bring with you is a direct offshoot of knowing the intended outcome of your meeting. You should always be ready to give samples—often and in abundance. Samples of a product many times sell themselves, and a prospect who asks for or tries a sample is already positively inclined toward the product you're selling. Never hold back as offering product and information is something that shows you're there to be of service to a customer. Important supporting materials could also include references, testimonials, research and any news articles pertinent to your offering, as well as return on investment (ROI) information.

And finally, always go into a sales call in the correct mental state. Be in the moment. What happened yesterday is over. What's going to happen tomorrow is still to come. If something other than the sales call is on your mind, step back and collect yourself before you commence the meeting; your customer should have no idea that there is anything going on in your life at that moment other than the meeting that is taking place. What that person needs before any sale takes place is your full and undivided attention. If you don't offer it, you may not get the chance to offer anything else.

CHAPTER 5

ENGAGEMENT

"What you chase will run." That quote applies to dating, it applies to sales, and it applies to the next step in the selling cycle: engagement.

If you're getting ready to meet with a prospect or client and you're fully prepared, you'll walk up to that person and show from the start that you're presenting yourself as being there to help. You'll be authentic, with no airs about you. You'll make a powerful first impression with a handshake and a look in the eye. You'll be 100% present, and you'll command respect like you own the place, even if you're in a place you've never visited before.

From the start, state your purpose. First and foremost, you are there to meet your prospect, begin to build a relationship, and learn about your prospect's business. If you're meeting a customer, even a longtime customer, you're there to learn more about the business. You are there to solve problems for your customer and be of service. The only way you can effectively do what you need to do is to fully engage, to listen and to learn. When the time is right, be completely honest about how what you have to offer can solve a particular problem. Let the customer know—via your words and actions—that no one in the world is more important at that moment to you or to your company.

I had a Border Collie named Griff who was the four-legged embodiment of engagement. I could wake him at 4:00 in the morning or roust him from a nap at sundown and he would be instantly ready to move livestock. No matter the weather, no matter how daunting the task, no matter how far away from home he was, no matter when he would next eat—when Griff knew it was time to work, he didn't let anything get in the way of his giving 100%.

Griff was lightning fast, getting ahead of the herd of sheep like he'd been shot out of a rifle. He didn't chase the livestock because he overtook them all in seconds. He would work until his pads were raw. He would work until he collapsed. He lived to move livestock and to serve me as his handler. He was fully engaged in what he was doing.

And so was I.

While Griff was serving my needs, I made sure I was serving his. It was important that I never pushed Griff to the point where his pads would get sore or he'd become exhausted. Griff was a special dog, and it was my obligation to him that, long before anything bad happened to him, I would give him a soft pat on the head and speak calmly to him: "That'll do."

When he heard that message, Griff would relax.

We were a great team because we were both fully engaged in what we were doing, we were both there to help each other, and what came out of it was a special relationship that I remember every day.

CHAPTER 6

RAPPORT

Developing rapport with a prospect can sometimes be difficult. The two of you aren't necessarily getting together for a social visit, even if you get along well; you're getting together because business called upon the two of you to do so. As long as you keep that fact in mind, you should have no problem developing rapport with the other party.

It's really all about reading the verbal and non-verbal communication of the person with whom you're dealing. If the person speaks quickly, make an effort to speak quickly yourself (or, at the very least, don't slow down the conversation). Conversely, if the person is highly contemplative about choosing his or her words, you may want to tap the brakes on how quickly you respond. Lean forward when the customer does, use similar hand gestures, and always look that person in the eye. These are small things that may come naturally to you, but as long as you're conscious of the situation, you'll soon make these verbal and non-verbal communications as natural a part of your sales presentation as the initial handshake.

I, for one, am very big on mirroring and matching what my prospect is doing, semi-mimicking hand gestures and matching the person's demeanor. It's not inauthentic to mirror and match, but it can come off that way if you're not doing the other important things, like finding areas of alignment, matching eye contact, paying attention, and reacting non-verbally to comments made by that person. Laugh when a story is funny, wince when a story involves pain. Be natural, sure, but don't forget what brought you there.

You're there to serve the person with whom you're speaking.

> Developing rapport with people is not unlike getting used to a horse. Horses are beautiful, stately animals, but they sure can be ugly when they have people on their backs they don't like. A person needs to develop a bit of a relationship with a horse before asking the horse to support his weight or the person is going to be bucked off and land in the dirt before he can say, "Hi-yo Silver, away!"
>
> In farm sales, we don't have to worry about getting bucked off a horse. But we do everything we can to avoid "getting the gate."

When I started to bring the mentality that I was serving other people to my sales career, I realized that I could talk to anyone and find rapport. It doesn't take long to learn a person's interests outside of work; some people read a lot of books, others like a particular kind of music, some have hobbies as diverse as stamp collecting or skydiving. I have learned that I don't have to be terribly interested in many of my customers' hobbies in order to introduce some small talk that picks up on a conversation we may have had during an earlier visit, a phone call, or even an e-mail exchange. I just have to find that little piece of information that allows us to connect—that little something that we have in common. That lone commonality could be as distant or unique as the fact that you both rode motocross cycles in the 1970s or you both have kids who've hiked to the top of Mount Kilimanjaro.

In my case the conversation that starts with a shared interest does indeed always come back to work. No matter who I'm meeting or what the situation is or how the conversation starts, my customers and I all wind up on the subject of the optimum health of their dairy cows. That's why I'm there. That's why the customer is talking to me. We both know it and that's why, in fairly short order, we get down to the business at hand.

Being of service to my customers means that I need to show them I care as much about that end goal as they do. I can't get to that point in the relationship by saying the right thing; I can only get to that point by doing the right thing. Do the right thing with customers from introduction to final handshake, and you'll have a rapport with each one that will keep the conversation going for years.

CHAPTER 7

DISCOVERY

Once you're aligned with your customer and you've developed a rapport, you can move into the discovery phase of your selling venture. You've already gained comfort in the selling situation, but now is when you can unearth the way you can help your customer. Now is the time to understand your customer's goals, concerns, and potential problems as they pertain to reaching the ultimate goal.

It's a terrific chance to probe for a specific need, an opportunity to find out if there's something more that your customer has held back, hasn't yet revealed. Keep in mind that this is a two-way street; a prospect who's comfortable at this point is going to start exposing some verbal and non-verbal buying signals like handling and spending a bit of time with one particular product or asking you some detailed questions about it.

I have learned over the years that people are often vague about what they want or need. They'll say they want a new screwdriver or a new car, but what is the problem they're really trying to solve? Once they start answering those questions—and start asking questions of their own—the relationship between the two of you really starts to mesh. Does this person just want a screwdriver to keep in the junk drawer? Or will he use it every day on the job? Does this person just want four wheels and an engine? Or will the vehicle be hauling three kids, four dogs, and five coolers full of food up to the cabin every weekend? Help people express what they really, truly aim to achieve with the purchase, and you will be serving them to the fullest.

> **You may tell people you're in sales, but the work you're really engaged in is helping people fill a need or desire; you're there to solve a problem. Keep that in mind every time you meet a customer.**

You can ask open, general questions as you present yourself and your company. Probe for specific needs, re-state the needs, and always check for agreement. Ask the simple question: "Does that make sense to you?" If you get an unsure expression in response, you may want to backtrack. If you get an enthusiastic thumbs-up in response, you are well on your way to satisfying a real need.

Let's say a person has come into your dealership and says he wants a car—make it your mission to find out more. Draw him out. Get him talking. Help him lead you, and you'll be leading him toward what he really wants. Plus, you'll certainly be serving him, allowing him to take an objective view of what he really needs. That sort of leadership will make you invaluable. Why does this person want a car? What is he going to do with it? Does he need extra horsepower? Less horsepower? How long does he intend to keep the car? Does he plan to sell it or hand it off to someone else in his family? Does he really need four-wheel drive? Is the color of the truck important to him? How about amenities? Go ahead and probe for specific needs and never forget that people like to talk about themselves: people largely enjoy telling others what they like and dislike and are willing to drill down (with your help) to the point where they answer for themselves exactly what they want—and that's when and how you can serve them.

Finding agreement is key. I make sure I don't just expect that one of my customers is going to pay me for the same dairy rations in the same form year after year; times change, situations change, the livestock we're trying to keep healthy change. When I'm in the discovery phase, I ask questions in order to uncover problems or concerns that need to be addressed. Then I re-state the needs as I look for agreement: "Did I hear you correctly when you said you're working with a lot of cows who are lactating for the first time?" "Does what I just told you I can do make sense to you?" "So, what I hear you say is that your herd will be 50 percent bigger two years from now—let's start making plans now so we're ready when that time comes."

Repeating your customer's words is always a great way to set up the question that can allow you to check for agreement. I had a wonderful experience when I was working in agronomy in Florida and met with an orange grove owner who had a very specific need: "You mentioned that you want to cut costs, correct?" I asked.

"That's right," was his response.

"So, if our fertilizer additive allows you to use less fertilizer, thereby saving money, and still get the same level of production…would you be interested in that?" I inquired. I made a point to repeat statements that my prospect had said before and then put a question at the end in order to get a response.

There's another important consideration for Florida citrus growers, one that is unique to the state. In Florida's Everglades, the water table is very high, and fertilizer can easily get to that water table and wash away. Not only is that a waste of fertilizer and a waste of money, it's also an environmental concern that growers are always trying to mitigate. So, improving efficiency hits growers positively by cutting costs and by lessening their businesses' environmental impact.

When I started working down there, I had no idea about that concern; only after asking questions and listening to what those experienced growers told me did I fully realize the importance of water run-off to everyone in the state.

Asking questions (and getting answers in the affirmative) is a great way to share information and bring the buying decision to a positive resolution. The practice helps you find agreement and allows you to come off without looking like a know-it-all or an overbearing presence. It allows you to lead the customer and rolls out the carpet for the person across the table to re-express goals (or perhaps express goals that have been repressed so far) and verbalize the actual solution.

"Tell me more about that," is a personal favorite. The phrase is a great way to dig deeper and show a genuine interest in what the person across the table is expressing. Say that often enough to a customer, and you'll begin to enlarge the need. Make sure you and your customer are absolutely in sync by getting ready to re-state or allow the other person to re-state. "So let me get this right…" or "Let me make sure I understand," are tremendous ways to introduce a re-statement and open the floor to clear up any possible discrepancies between what you've heard before and what your customer is trying to tell you.

It's amazing how often a buyer doesn't always express exactly what he or she needs until a conversation about that need really develops and takes shape.

When you're in a position to enlarge the need, you need to be substantive 100% of the time; this is no time for small talk. Don't derail the path to the sale. Recognize where the conversation is going and go with it until you're ready to say: "I think we have something that might help you."

Another way you can always be of service to your customer is by looking out for costs. The person you're meeting with will appreciate that you're keeping an eye on the budget. That's because costs are an existential threat to any business or even a household.

Hey, a business that runs out of money and closes down will never be a repeat customer, right? Same with a household.

Letting someone know you can cut his or her costs is a tremendous way to enlarge the need. For instance, if you can cut costs and maintain efficiency—"If I can cut your costs and still deliver the output you've told me you have to have, would you be interested?"—your customer will recognize your value and appreciate the fact that you're looking out for the budget as well as the need that absolutely must be met.

When you get to the point where you and the customer have good rapport, where you're aligned on the general need that your product or service is going to fulfill, it's time to really stress the impact of the need. As I stated earlier, "Tell me more about that" is a phrase that's perfect at many points of the sales process because it allows the customer to keep getting deeper into his or her needs. Coming on the heels of the budget discussion, it's very likely that the customer will expound on how you're helping him meet payroll or even stay in business.

CHAPTER 8

SOLUTION PRESENTATION

Just like "So let me get this right…" or "Let me make sure I understand…" earlier in the conversation, "Tell me more about that" is a phrase that a salesperson who goes into the job with a servant's heart can use to ensure there is no misunderstanding at all about what the customer wants, what he's really looking to achieve with the purchase. It's the last thing that needs to be said before you've exhausted the subject, making sure there's absolute alignment before moving forward into the solution presentation.

Here is the point where the conversation moves from the past and the present into the future. Now is the time when all you've learned turns into an offering that only you can present.

Even when I'm dealing with dairy producers that I've been selling to for years, I never present a solution before putting forth the effort to learn every concern, every issue, every goal, every last thing that is on each producer's mind. There's always news. Recall that a dairy cow can produce milk for only a certain number of lactations. There are a lot of demands on her body during that time, and that's why the nutrition I am providing has to be the best it can possibly be for all the cows. It has to be a ration that features all the correct levels of nutrients and is perfectly balanced for the production that the producer and I seek. When putting together the ration, I need to take into account the weather and the cow's physiology as well as the forage quality in the area.

Indeed, the cow pie doesn't lie. There's a lot of information for me at this point in the selling process, and it can only be learned when I strap on the boots, wander the pen, and get knee-deep in everything a cow leaves behind. Is she using everything she eats? Or is part of what she eats going all the way through her system unused and winding up on the floor of the pen? I need to know that before I can make a recommendation because no random combination of feeds will ever do for a dairy cow to stay healthy and produce effectively.

If I didn't take the time to learn everything I could from the producer and from his cows, the cows would likely fall short of meeting requirements. If that were the case, I would have come up short on presenting the proper solution as well as meeting the challenge—in its entirety—of keeping the dairy cows healthy and producing at their best over their lactating period. Only once I have all the information, right down to whatever I discover in the cow pies, do I step forward with the solution I present to a dairy producer.

> **Incredibly, many salespeople make the presentation of a solution the first step—the very first step—of their sales process. Before finding anything out about a customer, about that person's concerns or plans or needs, a salesperson will pull out a brochure. Without knowing what needs or desires have to be met, a salesperson will show off a product's specs or play up how a product performs in conditions that are often completely different than the conditions his or her prospect has in mind. Why do so many salespeople do this? Because they're simply selling what they have instead of solving a problem or fulfilling a need.**

Think about this: Let's say you work in a ski shop and a fit-looking, athletic young person walks up to you and wants to buy a pair of skis. What do you do? How do you react? It's important—vital—to know some information first. For instance, does this person wish to be a casual skier? Or is this person dreaming of starring in mogul skiing videos? Will this person be skiing frequently? Or is this person going to ski just a few days every year? Does this person have a desire to ascend to an expert level, acquiring a season pass, and spending every winter hitting the slopes as often as possible? Or is this person happy to stay at the intermediate level, skiing moderately challenging slopes during an annual vacation to the mountains? A little knowledge goes a long way toward making you invaluable to your customer.

What jumping to the solution presentation shows is that the sales-person hasn't taken the time or put in the effort to learn the challenge that the customer is facing. Preparation, engagement, rapport, and discovery have all been excused in the name of a fast sale, which can only come off as a hard sell à la the proverbial used car salesperson in the plaid polyester sport coat and the tie as wide and colorful as a sailboat's spinnaker.

It's infuriating, it's a shortsighted way to sell, and it reveals that the salesperson isn't being of service but rather just trying to make a snappy dollar.

Jumping directly to the solution presentation is often ineffective and disqualifying, as it reveals a severe lack of awareness and an acute inability to learn some small, single thing about a potential customer. Remember that there's always more to know, even about something as pedestrian as a person's vacation plans.

Here's a great example of a little knowledge that could go a long way: I have a friend who owns a farm in Kansas, where he grows lots and lots of corn. A corn seed salesman called my friend one day and asked if he could set up a meeting. My friend said sure, and they set a time. As soon as the corn seed salesman showed up, "the sell" was on. The salesman rattled on about the new product he had, that this particular corn seed was better than any before it. He pulled out charts and raved about the corn seed's off-the-chart yield and the fabulous germination rates. The salesman went over one feature after another after another.

"Sounds impressive," my friend said quietly as he reviewed the data.

"It'll change the way you farm," the salesman said enthusiastically.

"Indeed, it would," my friend replied as he looked up. "And that's the problem."

The salesman looked at him with a furrowed brow, completely perplexed.

"You see..." said my friend as he put the salesman's information down on his desk. "My brother and I see each other once a year, every year. We meet in Hawaii for the first two weeks of October. It's the most important two weeks of the year for me. It's the reason why I work so hard. It's also the reason why I need a shorter-season variety of corn seed." My friend looked down at the salesman's information sitting on his desk and got in the last word: "Yours won't do."

If the salesman had a shorter-season variety available, it didn't matter; he'd already compromised his credibility by going straight to the solution presentation. Salespeople who refuse to rush a sale—whether to meet a quota or some other reason—are 49 percent more successful in making the sale and also wind up selling about 35 percent more when they make the sale.[1] Had this particular corn seed salesman taken the time to find some alignment with my friend, he may not have had to "sell," but rather match what he had to offer with my friend's needs.

There's a long-standing view that the sales relationship is somewhat adversarial, that the salesperson is on one side of the table trying to take advantage of the customer who sits on the other side. My philosophy is that I NEVER think that way of the sales relationship I have with any customer, and that's been a key to my success. I employ the term, "Mutually beneficial, sustainable business relationship" instead in my effort to describe how I work with customers. In my mind, we are both on the same side of the table, with our sleeves rolled up, working together to meet a challenge and come to an agreement wherein both parties benefit equally from doing business together. Only in this scenario will the salesperson/customer relationship be sustainable for the long term, which should be the goal.

The solution presentation is not necessarily when you explain the technology or the features your product or service has; it's the time to present the proverbial puzzle piece, the one that perfectly fits the concerns or desires your customer has brought to you. As you're putting your solution on display, continue to ask yourself, "So what?" What needs do your product or service satisfy? Highlight those needs and how your solution answers them. During the solution presentation, keep asking yourself the question, "So what?" Don't stop. Never stop. "So what?" is the most important question in sales.

Why? Because if you can't answer that question time and time and time again, you do not have a solution that you're ready to offer. It's okay to admit that you don't have a solution "at this time." It can work in your favor, actually, to retreat, find a solution at a later time, and get back to your customer. The customer will appreciate the extra effort, honesty, and stick-to-it-ive-ness much more than receiving a product or service that doesn't absolutely answer the stated need and/or desire.

Finally, when it comes to presenting the solution, ALWAYS under-promise and over-deliver. The best words a salesperson can hear when following up with a client are: "What you sold me is better than I ever expected it to be."

CHAPTER 9

AGREEMENT

I f you've followed every step spelled out so far in this book and you've presented the solution, you likely won't have any trouble coming to agreement. That's because agreement is the result of your making your case, certainly not the result of your pressuring the person across the table from you, like the two of you are adversaries. Agreement should come so naturally that you barely notice you've reached it, that you're just about to make the sale, so be direct and confident, get straight to the point, and check for buying signals that are verbal and non-verbal.

> One of the key non-verbal buying signals is eye contact. It's important throughout the selling process and especially important for you to understand in the agreement phase, because it means that the customer is "with" you as you're on the cusp of the sale.

If your customer is making eye contact with you during the engagement, rapport, and discovery stages of your selling journey, it's very likely that the person will enthusiastically respond to your solution presentation by handling the product or brochure, looking at features, asking about benefits—in short, the person will be fully engaged when you most want him to be.

> If any pressure exists at this point in the selling process, if either you or the person you're talking to isn't comfortable, go back to the discovery step and tread the path again; chances are you'll learn something vital that will more easily pave your way to agreement. It's okay to show you're human and admit that something is not quite right—"I feel like I may have missed something here."
>
> But if agreement exists, STOP EVERYTHING YOU'RE DOING and move on to details, logistics, and logical next steps. Hand off the product, put together the purchase agreement, set a delivery date. Whatever the logical next step is, move to it immediately. Far too often a salesperson keeps selling, perhaps in an attempt to reinforce that the customer has made a good choice or perhaps in an ill-advised and unprofessional effort to up-sell. Few things in the buying process are more annoying for the person making the purchase than coming to an agreement and then having the salesperson move the proverbial goalposts. Once you reach agreement, the selling stops. Period. No questions asked.

There is a definitive reason I use the term "gaining agreement" and eschew the term "closing the sale." In fact, I suggest you never again use "closing the sale" or even think in those terms as you continue your career. Why? "Closing" implies that you are wrapping something up, completing it, that it's done...as in *finished*. If you aspire to exemplify the servant's heart, you have to believe that the exact opposite is true. Gaining agreement is not the end of something; it's the beginning.

For any variety of reasons, the average company loses 10 to 30 percent of its customers every year.[2] This fact as well as the fact that retaining current customers is 6 to 7 times less costly than acquiring new ones[3] might help to convince you to accept this sort of a mindset about each and every customer you presently have.

Once agreement on a sale has happened, you have the opportunity to show your customer that you're going to do whatever is necessary to ensure that the product or service performs in a way you both want it to. Even if you're selling something that is typically seen as a one-time purchase—not normally a product that is sold once a week or once a month, for instance—don't think the sale is ever "closed." Keep the relationship with your customer open, always open. You never know when more business is going to walk through that open door, whether it's an unexpected repeat sale or possibly a referral. You are in the business of managing relationships, not selling products or services. Never forget that, and you will have so many more sales than if you're always going through your workday trying to "close sales."

Moreover, instead of your sales work feeling like a stressful struggle without much meaning beyond making a living, it will feel fun, natural, and rewarding on every level.

Now, one of the true passions of the life that I love to lead is hiking. I have been a wilderness explorer since I was a young boy, and my love of the outdoors has grown ever since. A number of years ago, I began employing llamas to carry packs of gear for my family, friends, and me when we went out on multi-day hikes. More recently I have been hiking with goats—pack goats—to carry our gear and have found these animals to be amazing workers and companions, which I'll explain more later in the book. Like a customer who's had a bad experience, pack goats will remember a bad experience and take it out on you in the future. They will be less enthused to carry future loads and will harbor suspicion about your motives and how you'll treat them. It's nearly impossible to re-gain the trust of a pack goat who feels he's been wronged.

Customers are no different: One bad experience dealing with too much sales pressure can sour the relationship so that it will take a long time and lots of effort to mend. Worse, it could permanently damage the relationship. Always be mindful of the experience your customer is having and don't be afraid to ask about it either. I have many times asked, "How are you feeling about this?" or, "Are you comfortable as we're proceeding here?" These are very natural questions and good ways to start a dialogue that can strengthen the rapport and agreement you have with your customer, bringing your relationship to a higher level.

CHAPTER 10

OBJECTIONS

I f the customer has any objections at all, she will present them now. It's important that you do not shy away from objections here, but rather welcome them. Objections are not necessarily negative, and if you think about them as unsatisfied needs and respond with something like, "That's a good point" or "I'm glad you brought that up," you'll gain even more credibility. The fact is that responding to an objection at this point allows you to continue to move toward a true Needs Satisfaction Solution for your customer.

Don't be defensive, don't be too proud, don't jump to conclusions, and don't EVER disagree or argue when a prospect has any kind of objection.

Objections can occur even with a repeat customer, based on changing circumstances and unknown information, just as they can be raised by an animal with whom you've had a great working relationship. When I was a sheep rancher in Montana, I recall checking on my flock in the late spring. Lambing season was over, and my Great Pyrenees dog, Pearl, was charged with protecting the ewes and their lambs, so I was surprised and quite upset to see her lying by herself some distance away. I set my jaw, changed direction, and pointed at my dog. I was just about to scold Pearl, so mad I was at her behavior— at her not following the method that she knew and had performed so often in the past—that I could feel my forehead getting hot and starting to perspire.

But then I noticed it! That's when I saw what she saw—exactly what I needed to see...

Right behind Pearl I saw a singular ewe who was in labor. Pearl's instincts had told her that this particular ewe was the most vulnerable to predators in the area and based her decision upon that knowledge.

My mood changed immediately as I saw the situation from Pearl's point of view. My voice, because my throat had gone suddenly dry in my brief fit of anger—was a little scratchy when I said: "Very good, Pearl. Very good." I started to smile as I saw Pearl keep her powerful body next to the laboring ewe. "Good girl." I empathized with Pearl's thinking and immediately admired her judgment. She hadn't simply followed the tried-and-true method that Great Pyrenees have followed for generations; she assessed a unique situation and made a decision based on what she felt was best for the ewe in labor as well as the entire flock. She had attained mastery.

Once the ewe had given birth, she and her lamb joined the flock, and Pearl got back on patrol, calmly guarding the animals and sniffing the wind for traces of trouble.

I smiled at the scene and turned back, thankful that I hadn't snapped at Pearl as soon as I saw her separated from the herd. Had I done so I would have been the one in the wrong as Pearl was doing exactly what she knew she had to do. If Pearl had caught my wrath when she was obviously doing the right thing, I would have permanently damaged the relationship I had with her, a relationship upon which both my professional and personal lives were invested.

The application of this story to your sales career is that if your customer raises an objection you can either be defensive—objecting to the objection—or you can immerse yourself in the objection. Take the first road, and you'll very likely move the process and the relationship backward. Choose the second road, and you'll understand the objection from someone else's point of view. Then you'll be able to work through the objection together until the concern is put completely to rest. Then, and only then, will you put the objection behind you and keep it where it belongs—in the past.

Pearl guarding her sheep

Selling is based on relationships, and those relationships must always be nurtured. No one is going to buy from you—and feel good about it—if that person's trust in you has been compromised. It's much the way Pearl would not have maintained the trust she'd had in me if I'd bruised the relationship that I'd cultivated over years with her.

I do have a few final thoughts on the selling cycle I have detailed here, things that I need to impart before I take you *Beyond The Method* and help you pursue mastery in the sales profession. The first is that I live by a creed that I call "Feed the Relationship." What I mean by that is that I am constantly trying to give more and more to the selling relationship. That can be in the form of time or product or simple above-and-beyond-the-call effort; no matter what I'm engaged in with my customers, I make the honest effort to give more to the relationship than I ever take away.

> Just about anyone can engage in "informational" selling. Just about every brochure or website can too! I've come to learn that "informational" selling is all about I: what I have for you, what I am offering you, what I am selling and at what price. People who base a sales pitch on simple information are talking about themselves and what it is that they're selling.
>
> Conversely, "inspirational" selling is all about the customer and that customer's needs. Inspirational selling is never about the salesperson's needs.

If I were selling penny candy, I would put so much effort into it that people would feel they got their money's worth if they'd paid twice as much for it. Same thing if I were selling Ferrari Enzo sports cars.

These road missiles go for more than $1,000,000 apiece, so buyers certainly expect a lot for their money…if I were selling them, I would make sure my customer drove away convinced that he'd had a buying experience that was worth at least $1,000,001. Give more than you take, and you'll always be feeding the relationship.

Another way to feed the relationship is to keep your word, even when it involves the most seemingly mundane of topics. I was having a meeting with a prospect a number of years ago: the meeting went well—it was easy to see from the beginning that he was going to hear me out but not make a purchase on the spot. As I was gathering my materials and getting ready to leave his office, the guy piped up and said, "I like your hat."

"Really," I shrugged as I pulled at the brim of the baseball cap bearing my company's name and logo. "I'll send you one if you'd like."

"That would be great," he replied in an even tone.

I got home and went directly to my office. After rummaging around a bit, I found a hat like the one I'd been wearing, Then I grabbed an empty box, placed the hat into it, scribbled the guy's address on a label, and dropped the box in the mail the following day.

A few days later the phone rang. "I got your hat," said the guy I'd met with a few days earlier.

"Oh, terrific," I responded. "How does it look on you?"

"Dunno," said the guy. "I don't wear hats. My wife tells me I look goofy in them."

I was perplexed. If he didn't wear hats why did he graciously accept my offer to send him one? I waited a beat because I didn't know how to respond, but as I cleared my throat the guy cut in. "Just wanted to let you know you got the account."

I was floored. I got the account? Just like that? A simple $7 hat had turned into a $27,000 account for me? Indeed, it had. The guy and I talked a little further, moving straight into the agreement phase, discussing logistics and schedules. But before we got off the phone, he told me that he'd met with two other salesmen and that they'd both promised to send him a hat, but neither one did. "If they failed to do something as insignificant as sending me a hat, what else would they fail to do for me?" he said before the call ended.

> **"I would rather be accused of breaking precedents than breaking promises."** —*John F. Kennedy*

Obviously, that chapter in my sales career has had quite an impact on me simply because I recall the emotion I was feeling as I put the hat into the box, addressed it, and dropped it into the mail: it was pride. I recall thinking that I'd told the guy I'd send him a hat and there was no way that I would give him a reason to say anything but good things about me. I had made a promise and I had fulfilled it because of the pride I take in every aspect of my work. I know that if I do the right thing in my professional life the right thing will happen for my customer and me in the end.

It's almost like visualization. Great athletes and great actors visualize their performance before it happens as a way of seeing success happen before success is a reality. Superstar ski racer Lindsey Vonn was famous for visualization; we saw her before races, seemingly in a trance as she stood still and shifted her weight, bobbed her head, stuck out her hands—all in an effort to visualize the course down which she was about to race. Visualization was one of the tools she used to find the perfect path from the top of the mountain to the bottom. She was a prime example of an athlete who was "in the moment," who had nothing else on her mind when she was on the course than what she was doing on the course. She never let what happened in the last race affect how she would perform in her present race. Injuries—and she had many—only served as the next obstacle to overcome. She would put her mind to getting healthy again because that was what she needed to do on that particular day. "What happened yesterday happened," she might say. "What will happen tomorrow will happen tomorrow." What's happening right now is what she knew she could control. She gave everything she had at every moment to her sport, and she did that so well she became the most decorated competitive skier the world has ever known.

Lindsey Vonn's ski career was the athletic personification of Dr. Wayne Dyer's precept that absolutely nothing should distract you from what you're doing right now. Hailed by some as the "Father of Motivation," Wayne Dyer was a bestselling author and speaker who has been a big influence on me for years. One of the stories he liked to tell centered around an event in China that people attend for one single reason: to drink tea.

That's right. People come to drink tea just for the experience of drinking tea.

Anywhere else in the world, people drink tea and talk to friends. In other places and other times, people drink tea and listen to music. Or drink tea and drive to work. But the goal at this event is to remove all obstacles between the human being and something as simple as a cup of tea.

The point is, whatever you're doing, you should concentrate on what you're doing and enjoy what you're doing while you're doing it. Bring that mentality to your selling career, be in the moment when you're engaging with your customer, enjoy the moment as it's happening, never forget that you are there to be of service to the person across the table from you, and you will find that you are bringing a servant's heart to your selling career.

PART TWO

GOING BEYOND
THE METHOD

CHAPTER 11

DISCOVERING MY SERVANT'S HEART

There's nothing like a blizzard to disrupt everything. Entire cities close down, electricity goes out, tree branches fall across roads and sometimes smash people's cars. Metropolitan areas can go completely dark—literally and figuratively—and economic activity grinds to a halt everywhere except at a ski resort and a tow truck business.

That was especially the case back during the winter of 1995-96. The Internet was infant technology, and connections were not at all common in peoples' residences. In order to connect to the Internet at home, a person would have to plug the computer into a phone line, direct the computer to make a phone call, wait for the buzzing and pulsing sounds to abate, and then sit there for a few minutes while an America Online home page showed up on the screen line by line by line in low resolution. And that was the case when the weather outside was perfect! The words "text" and "friend" had yet to be used as verbs, people still watched movies at home after running off to the video store to rent VHS tapes, and the tech world had yet to hail the introduction of Sony's PlayStation and Windows '95. A few people had big, clunky cellular phones back then, but we generally needed landlines.

I was living in my beloved Montana at the time and had just started my sales career with a company that manufactured feed for livestock. I logged a lot of miles back then, driving all over the western part of The Treasure State. My job was to sell to the ranchers who work millions of acres of land and thousands of head of beef cattle to feed America. In the world of sales, I was still a bit of a newbie who was finding his way in the business.

But I wasn't going to make any sales calls on this particular day. It was just a few weeks into the year—probably January, maybe February—when a huge blizzard blew through. In its wake, the storm left at least a couple feet of snow. When the sky cleared, the mercury dropped and the temperature was somewhere below zero. A white blanket covered the landscape as far as the eye could see, and drifts were halfway up the walls on the south sides of barns and houses.

For a few hours after I awoke, I wasn't sure what the day was going to bring. Probably a little paperwork. Certainly no driving to meet any ranchers. No sales. The entire Rocky Mountain West had gotten hit by the storm, and it appeared everyone living in the time zone was going to spend the day—maybe the next few days—digging out.

No, I didn't make sales calls that day. I didn't even think about making sales calls. But the lesson I learned in the ensuing hours would transform my sales career forever and make me more successful than I ever thought I would become.

Here's how the morning played out...

I mulled a few things over, nothing terribly important, including the fact that I'd just recently splurged and gotten myself a Honda FourTrax 300. It was a bright red ATV that had four-wheel-drive, of course, and was considered at the time to have a mid-size engine. I had also ordered a snowplow kit that mounted under the frame, and I was just learning how to use it that winter.

The FourTrax did not have a winch—which I probably could have purchased and put onto the vehicle myself—but the plow itself had a lever that extended to the left of the driver's seat. All I had to do was pull back on the lever and the plow blade raised up. I could lock it in the "up" position and ride around, which I'd done quite a bit before the snow fell. I had also added a few luxuries to the four-wheeler like heated handle grips, which were really pleasant, and a heated throttle lever. Much like the throttle on a snowmobile, the four-wheeler's engine got gas when I pressed on a small lever with my right thumb while holding the right handle grip. The heated throttle was a welcome feature as just a short time spent applying pressure on the throttle and giving the engine gas could compromise the blood circulation in my digit and render it frozen no matter how good the gloves or mittens I was wearing.

Manipulating the snowplow itself was pretty easy. The lever that I could reach with my left hand allowed me to raise or lower the plow and I quickly realized that performing that action a number of times would result in a tremendous workout. I could change the angle of the blade by coming to a stop, hopping off the ATV, going to the front, pulling a pin, and moving the blade so I could roll snow to my left or my right. If need be, I could also set the blade in a way that I could push snow straight ahead, resulting in it rolling off to both my left and right.

The FourTrax had no windshield, so in the winter I would wear ski goggles, a warm hat, and a scarf or a neck gaiter. Along with the beard I sported during the cold months, I was able to keep my face fairly warm as I pulled the gaiter up over my nose. The rest of my body was also equipped for the cold of a Montana winter morning with long johns, jeans, Carhartt insulated coveralls, a thick jacket, and insulated gloves that were as thick as they could be while still affording me some dexterity. I anchored the whole outfit with Sorel boots that had felt liners. I looked like The Michelin Man waddling out to the barn, where I stored the FourTrax.

The four-wheeler stayed in the same area where we lambed out the sheep. It was quite cold in the barn, so I would warm the FourTrax engine with the same infrared heat lamp I used when the lambs were born. Just a quick thaw was all I needed to help the engine turn over.

At 300 ccs, the FourTrax was not super powerful. So, when we got a snow like we got that morning, I would try to give the four-wheeler a head start, then hit a pile or drift of snow on the run. Overall, it was really a lot of fun, but it could be hard work as I was still getting the hang of the plow and its capabilities. I plowed a path from the house to the barn and then a large area around the barn—the places where we always walked. It was important that we could easily access the hay bales, for instance, so that feeding the animals on our land didn't involve trudging through snow if that could be avoided.

We had a long gravel driveway, which presented a special kind of challenge. The lever to my left could raise or lower the blade, but I needed to hold the lever if I were to keep the snowplow's blade in place, hovering above the surface of the driveway. And that's what I needed to do so I didn't plow all the gravel off the driveway along with the snow. That could be quite a workout, especially with all the snow before me. I held the blade just an inch or two above the gravel, all the while steering the FourTrax with my right hand. When I was done, I had cleared a path out to the county road that was basically a skiff of snow sitting upon the gravel.

After I finished our driveway, I gave the FourTrax a little gas and reviewed the areas I'd just plowed, checking out my handiwork and making sure I hadn't missed anything. But as I did so I felt a little reluctant to call the job complete. Truth be told, riding along on that four-wheeler was a lot of fun. Even in below-zero temps, it's the next best thing to a trail ride.

As I was finishing up, I looked over at our neighbors' house. It was a gorgeous two-story wood structure that was home to a retired couple of Montana native ranchers named Russell and Rachel. They were great people. If the leather on a horse saddle could talk, its voice would sound like Russell's. A real John Wayne-like character, Russell was an impressive old-school rancher who'd done extremely well for himself raising Hereford Cattle. He hadn't gotten involved in oil or any other business during his career; he just stuck with what he knew, and that served him well.

Russell and Rachel were getting on in years, however, and were no longer active ranchers at all. They certainly weren't going to get outside and move the snow from this storm.

I regarded their house for a moment. They had a long, paved driveway and a barn area that was much like ours. "Are they going to wait for a plowing service to show up?" I thought to myself. After this storm, that could take days.

Or it could be minutes.

I revved the engine, turned the handlebars, drove over the cattle guard of our driveway and onto the county road, which didn't have any traffic on it at the time. I will never forget the thoughts going through my head and I drove my FourTrax over to the driveway next door: "I might as well do this. I'm all togged up. I'm having fun. I have no idea what sort of arrangements Russell and Rachel have made for snow removal after such a heavy blizzard." Doing what I was going to do just seemed natural, like there was no way I wasn't going to do it.

When I got to the spot where their driveway met the county road, I grabbed the lever of my snowplow with my left hand and lowered the blade of the plow as low as it would go; the paved driveway didn't call for quite the light touch that I'd had to display on my own driveway. Over the next 15 minutes I'd roll snow to one side of their driveway and then the other all the way to their garage. I cleared off their front walk in no time and couldn't help but notice Russell and Rachel stick their heads out the door. I idled the FourTrax, hopped off, removed the goggles from my eyes, and started toward our neighbors.

"We couldn't help but hear you out here. Thank you so much," Russell said with a big grin on his broad, weathered face.

Rachel was holding a coffee mug in her right hand and made a motion toward it with her left. "Come in for coffee and cookies," she insisted.

I demurred. I looked like a real live snowman with all the snow that had stuck to my face and clothing. As much as I appreciated the offer, it made no practical sense for me to enter their home as I was, take off all my outerwear, and allow the snow to melt on their floor. What kind of a guest would I be? Plus, I'd have to put the stuff on again after my visit was done.

There never was much activity over at their house, and I was pretty sure Russell and Rachel were excited about the prospect of hosting company, if only for a short bit. "Thanks so much," I said before I added: "Not right now. How about tomorrow?"

Our neighbors both smiled and nodded. Yes, that would be wonderful, they said before they closed the door.

I returned to my four-wheeler with every intention of heading back home and trying to get into some work. But then it hit me like it had hit Forrest Gump when he ran to the edge of Greenbow County: "I've come this far," I said to myself. "Why not keep going?" After all, I was really getting a feel for using the snowplow attachment on the FourTrax. Not only that, the bitter cold of the morning was having no effect on the joy I was feeling as I scooted and skidded around.

The property where we lived next to Russell and Rachel was on the outskirts of our small town of about 500 residents. The people who lived near us had acres and acres of rolling ranch land, and the spectacular Beartooth Mountains enlivened the panorama in the distance. My in-laws lived in what would be considered the downtown section. I thought about their house, then I thought about how I was getting better at manipulating snow with each pass. The great thing about the FourTrax—I'd come to realize—was that it was very agile, not at all like those behemoth ATVs with 1000 cc engines that would soon become common or a big pickup truck with a plow on the front. As such, I realized I was able to plow small sections within tight areas, like a sidewalk.

I'd just removed snow from Russell's and Rachel's front walk, and it was no wider than the sidewalk in front of my in-laws' house. With a shrug of my shoulders and a smile on my face, I rode my FourTrax to the end of my neighbors' driveway…and didn't go home.

Instead, I rode directly to my in-laws' house, quickly manipulated my blade, and removed the snow from their driveway with dispatch. Then I turned my attention to the sidewalk in front of their house and considered the postman's potentially difficult trudge in the coming days. In just a couple of passes I was able to clear that area and make at least part of the postman's route easier.

As I finished up, I remembered that my in-laws' neighbors, Joe and Jennie, had become friends of ours in recent years. They were so nice. My head involuntarily bounced up and down as if to say, "Yes." It only felt natural to do something nice for them as I plowed their driveway and sidewalk.

Of course, everyone could hear my four-wheeler going to work and would come outside and wave. Many would smile and yell, "Thank you," which I couldn't hear over the din but I certainly understood the sentiment. I rode around to the houses of a few other people I knew, plowed their driveways and sidewalks, and got much the same reaction from them.

When I got home, I hopped off the four-wheeler, dusted it off as best I could—it was caked with snow! Then I put it back into the barn, turned off the engine, and took it all in as I felt my smile widen and heard the tiny icicles on my beard break with the expression.

The confluence of two realizations had come together that morning. As much as I loved Montana, I had never thought of the state's sometimes-legendary snowfall as being a part of its charm; I'd always looked at blizzards as something I endured in order to enjoy the land, the wide-open spaces, and the bright blue canopy overhead that give the state its nickname of "Big Sky Country." But on this morning, I realized that snowstorms were nothing about which to be upset. They were, in fact, completely necessary in the arid Rocky Mountain West for so many reasons like providing drinking water and mitigating forest fires. These were things I knew and understood in an academic sense, but on this morning, I came to appreciate the snow I saw on the land as something more of a life-giving force than a disruption of a workday.

The second thing I realized was that removing snow wasn't much of a job to me. In fact, it was an empowering feeling to be able to clear so much snow so quickly with the help of my snowplow. Overall, I felt like I was getting the last word in an argument with Mother Nature.

When I walked back into our house, I felt a tinge of grief... ENTIRELY because the morning was over. Overall, I felt contented. I felt happy. I felt proud. I felt a strange and oddly satisfying mix of feelings.

I couldn't put my finger on exactly how I felt, but I do recall honestly regretting that my snow-clearing escapade was over. I was looking forward to the next time. I savored the mix of feelings I was experiencing and recall how novel it was for me; it didn't feel like I'd completed something I had to do for work, it didn't feel like work at all. But it didn't feel like charity either.

The feeling I experienced as I took off my boots is a feeling I remember to this day. I couldn't describe it at the time, but I know that if I had charged for the snow removal, I wouldn't have gotten the same feeling. I realized that I'd tapped in to something that I could bring forth in my work and my personal life for the rest of my days.

> It was years later that I would run across a quote by the actor Jim Carrey that best captured the feeling I had that morning: "How will you serve the world? What do they need that your talent can provide? That's all you have to figure out."

The satisfaction I felt as I finished my hours of snowplowing, I came to realize, was derived from my knowledge that I had displayed a servant's heart. Being of service to these people had given me a feeling that went beyond that of a job well done, beyond following a specific direction. I found meaning in what I'd done: I hadn't just plowed snow; I'd helped people.

There was a feeling of accomplishment that was hard to explain. It was a feeling of being worthwhile, of being appreciated and valued by other people. I started making a point to let people in when I was caught in traffic—not a common occurrence in Montana but it would be an opportunity I'd have often when we moved to Florida. I started appreciating time with my family, my friends, my customers, my dogs and other animals simply because I started to see myself through their eyes and wanted these others to have a positive feeling about what I saw.

In short, I looked for opportunities to put my servant's heart on display. That was something that would serve me well as I got traction in sales. It's probably more accurate to say that it's the very reason why I got my traction in sales.

But before I would make one more sales call—my first after discovering my servant's heart—I stopped by Russell's and Rachel's house for coffee and cookies. We talked about the weather, we talked about kids, we talked about Montana, we talked about the many wonderful things we've all been lucky enough to enjoy. It was a highly memorable visit, one that I treasure to this day.

CHAPTER 12

MY SERVANT'S HEART ON DISPLAY

I was in an interesting position at that point of my sales career. I was still relatively new to the profession, and I was doing okay. Perhaps that was because my company was just then expanding to western Montana, and every sale I made, every account I gained, was a 100% improvement over my company's sales in the area before they'd hired me.

But there was something more. My background was completely unique: I was a sheepherder who was transitioning to sales. Most of my clients were used to working with ranchers—or people who'd been ranchers or who'd worked with ranchers—to get the proper nutrition for their livestock. I wasn't a fellow "cowboy," I wasn't one of the "good ol' boys." I was a person coming into the business of beef nutrition sales with a few new ideas and unique perspectives. For instance, almost every rancher I encountered early in that phase of my career had the idea that a good vitamin and mineral program for their cows was to toss into the pasture some trace mineral salt blocks, which are basically 98% salt. A cow would have to lick that salt block 2,000 times to get a single ounce of consumption.

Now, a cow may like doing that. But spending all that time licking the salt block wasn't doing the cow much good and it certainly wasn't helping the ranchers get the most out of their cows.

I was introducing new, and more expensive, technology to the ranchers that consisted of loose-blended supplements that included much higher levels of vitamins and minerals—and not so much salt. At that time beef prices were low, and western Montana was experiencing a pretty severe drought. Times were tough for ranchers, so I had a couple strikes against me as I stepped to the plate and tried to sell my company's supplements.

Fortunately, my company had some terrific production trials and documentation that I could use to help present a very handsome return on investment equation to my prospective customers. In fact, the former head of the Montana Cattlemen's Association had been part of my company's study, so that endorsement was a big plus as I tried to convince ranchers that they should spend more on what I had to offer.

The training that I'd been given as I took on the sales position had been thorough and entirely worthwhile. I knew how to approach a customer, I knew the best ways to convince a customer to agree to try what I had to offer, I knew how to go about making the sale. What I didn't know then was that the training I'd received—"The Method"—made up only about 20 to 25 percent of the entire sales recipe.

> **"Your most unhappy customers are your greatest source of learning."**   —*Bill Gates*

But after my snowplowing experience, after I realized my servant's heart, I came to the conclusion that I could bring something more to the selling equation. I could bring the mentality that I wasn't just trying to sell something; I was presenting myself as being there to help these people.

The results—both tangible and intangible—once I started to bring this sort of thinking to my sales calls were so much better. I started telling myself every morning: "I'm going to go out and help someone today." I brought to the job the idea that I was there to understand my customer's needs and concerns, I was there to find solutions and help my customer realize those solutions, and, once I delivered those solutions, everything else would fall into place. Income. Referrals. Reputation. Everything. Bringing that mentality to sales calls made my job so much more enjoyable and made me such a better vendor to my customers that it was clear we had become business partners rather than salesman and buyer.

Basically, I was connecting with my clients on a more human level, and it was so much more natural than "trying to sell." It was also much more fun for me and, more important, I believe it was more fun for my customers as well.

One time after taking on this mentality in my sales career, I was talking to a rancher who was considering a temporary fencing project and I immediately offered a solution. In a previous professional iteration, I had worked with a fencing company based in Cody, Wyoming, and had had a really good experience with them. The quality of the company's fencing was certainly consistent with what the rancher needed, and I was confident that he'd find the price competitive.

My offering this information had nothing to do with beef nutrition. It had nothing to do with vitamins and minerals for the rancher's livestock. It had everything to do with my just wanting to help the guy. Sure enough, he called the Wyoming fence company. Following a short consultation, the company built a length of fence to test, the test went well, and the rancher wound up having a fence installed all around the perimeter of his property.

Another rancher once complained to me about his chainsaw. He was having to pull the starter dozens of times, pull the choke, prime it, let it rest, try it again—the rancher was fed up! I suggested a brand of chainsaw that had worked for me for years, gave the rancher the name of a guy who could demonstrate it, and got out of the way. A week later the rancher bought the chainsaw from my reference and was thrilled with the fact that he only had to pull the starter a time or two and the machine was humming.

The result? I was seen by these ranchers as something much more than a salesman or a vendor; I was a person they liked having around. I was a guy who offered solutions, and I hadn't even tried to "sell" something. Before I'd ever tried to sell these ranchers anything, they had already bought in to the idea that I was an asset to their businesses.

My own realization was that being that person—being someone whose presence is an asset—is what starts to make you important to your client. It's not part of any sales method. It can't be taught. It's entirely part of going *Beyond The Method.*

Do you employ such a mentality in your own sales career? Do you put a monetary value on even the smallest bit of advice or time you offer to a customer? Or do you offer to a customer what you know, what you care about, what you can recommend?

In short, are you making yourself an asset? Or are you just trying to sell something?

You don't need to experience an "Aha!" moment like I did on my Honda four-wheeler during that cold winter morning in Montana. You don't need to have some person, or some situation, point out to you what's missing in your sales career. You just need to find the way or ways that you can be helpful to your customers, offering them solutions to their problems.

And those solutions don't always have to do with what you're selling.

CHAPTER 13

A PACK GOAT'S PERSPECTIVE

My experience with pack goats has been one of the most eye-opening and rewarding parts of my life as a salesman, as a person, and as a lifelong hiker. Pack goats have added to and helped me live the life I am so happy to live.

A key ingredient of this life that I love is something I was exposed to years ago...

When I was 12 years old, my father took me on my first backpacking trip in Montana's spectacular Glacier National Park. To this day I will never forget the array of feelings I experienced as Dad and I drove to the trailhead and hit the trail, starting with nervousness about wildlife we might encounter and transitioning to awe as I saw one incredible vista after another. Climbing steep inclines or negotiating rough terrain were challenges I welcomed as I became more and more comfortable with the hike and evermore aware that I'd soon see something else that would take my breath away.

Now, this story is very personal to me and very important in my development as a person who's set out his vision of his life and strived every day to turn that vision into a reality. I do not live to work; I work so that I can live the life I see for myself, and a major part of that life was what I discovered on that day when I was 12 years old hiking with my dad. I was absolutely taken by the whole experience.

Backpacking and hiking are as much a part of me as the color of my eyes, as the lines on my face, as the hair on my head. It's not just a recreational endeavor for me—not just something I do and then move on to the next thing. It's part of who I am. When I'm not hiking in the backcountry, I've got a plan put together for my next trip. Some people are most at peace when they're fly-fishing or sailing or golfing or piloting a plane. I am most at peace with myself and the world as a whole when I'm on the trail or venturing off it.

It was an absolute coincidence that my purchasing a llama named Jasper while I was living in Montana became a part of my transition many years later to pack goats. Llamas are tremendous animals with gentle personalities, but they also are terrific guard animals. We got Jasper as a guard for our sheep, and he did a wonderful job fulfilling that charge.

One day I was packing 40 pounds of gear into a backpack for my next adventure, and I looked over at Jasper. Native to the Andes Mountains, llamas are tremendously agile for animals that can weigh more than 400 pounds and can carry as much as 80 pounds on their backs. They're beasts of burden, and they have been for centuries. I thought about my knees, my hips, my belief that carrying so much weight in my backpack would not add to the fun of being out on the trail.

That was when I decided it was time to give Jasper a second job.

I quickly grew to love hiking with Jasper. He just gave and gave and gave. He carried all of our heaviest gear and allowed me to carry lighter essentials. I appreciated everything about this impressive animal and would go on to buy a number of other llamas, training them and hiking with them and enjoying their company.

One day I was hiking with Jasper in the Beartooth Mountains. I spotted another group of hikers with a herd of four animals I didn't immediately recognize. They didn't look like llamas, but they weren't too different from llamas either. I was intrigued. The animals were smaller, they sported horns that sprouted from their heads, and they seemed very comfortable around the people in their group. I would soon learn that these animals were pack goats.

Jasper, my dual-purpose llama

Pack goats have been employed for centuries to carry loads in the spectacularly steep mountains of Iran and Tibet.[1] Along with dogs, goats were the first animals to be domesticated by humans more than 10,000 years ago.[2] They can often walk without a lead, they're cheaper to buy and keep than llamas, and yet they display a high level of service to people.

I couldn't stop thinking about these animals and learned that a gentleman named John Mionczynski—a Wyoming biologist and naturalist—is considered the "father of goat packing" in the United States. I read his 1992 book The Pack Goat a few times and learned that goats had started being used for packing in North America just a few years before the book came out. The book taught me about how bottle-feeding goats from the moment they're born means you bond with the goat and the goat learns to trust you. There is training involved as the goats grow up, and, properly trained, goats essentially become a pet you can count on out in the backcountry, able to go places like rocky fields that even llamas can't go. It appeared from my research that pack goats might become a part of my hiking team in the future.

That was about the time that circumstances sent me to Florida, where the hiking is scarce, and my lifestyle would change dramatically. My recreation there largely revolved around motorcycles and beach visits, and any llamas vs. goats debate that had been going on in my head didn't come up again until I returned to the Rocky Mountain West.

I was extremely happy to get back to the mountains and dived back into the lifestyle here. My wife and I bought some land, we built a house, and we settled into the whole construct of mountain living. I resumed my career in sales—this time with a dairy nutrition company—and fell back in love with the high peaks and low nightly temperatures. Life was good, save for the llamas vs. goats conundrum I was dealing with in my head. I didn't know if I should get llamas like I'd had in Montana or goats like the ones that I simply couldn't get off my mind.

Before I could make the decision, however, other issues came to the fore. It was the fall of 2013, and a series of unexpected, profoundly powerful events took place, culminating in the passing of my brother. Much reflection came as a result—my brother was only two years older than I—and my own thoughts started to center on unrealized dreams. I wondered if my brother had had any when he passed away and then turned my thinking inward. He'd been professionally successful. He'd never displayed any regrets. But did he pass with any unrealized dreams?

More germane to the time and the situation: did I have any unrealized dreams?

Indeed, I did.

Like books on a shelf that go unread, collecting dust, unrealized dreams don't do anything until the dreamer pulls them off the shelf, wipes off the dust, and opens them up. I had to admit to myself that I had a couple of dreams that I'd yet to tackle. Not many. I was pretty happy with the way things were in my life and the life we were making for ourselves back in the mountains. But losing a brother shines a more concentrated light on everything.

And that's why it was fitting that I was doing some work outside one day shortly after my brother's passing, thinking of my brother, thinking of my dreams, when I heard his voice. I didn't pretend I'd heard it. I didn't hope I'd heard it. I'd heard it. "Pal!" He called me "Pal," never by my name. "Pal! If you want yer dang goats, get yer dang goats!"

At first, I was scared to have heard my brother's voice so clearly, but then I smiled. I smiled broadly. It was him. It was his voice. It was like he'd heard my internal discussions about whether I should get llamas or goats for hiking companions. Finally, with the help of my late brother, I'd come to the decision.

I ran into the house and told my wife about getting the message from my brother. "Sweetheart," I said with a smile on my face. "I'm getting pack goats."

She endorsed my decision immediately, and a few days later we were in Nebraska picking out two goats that we'd name Wilson and Bert, a tribute to Mount Wilson and Mount Elbert, which features the highest point in Colorado. I was so impressed by what I learned from the breeder who sold us the goats, how the animals have a tremendous work ethic and how they perform their duties with dignity and pride. All they ask in return is a few kind words and a pat on the head.

> Pack goats can be almost machine-like in their ability to keep going, like my trusty pickup truck that's never let me down. But one should not overdo it! These animals who are carrying all the weight are also developing a relationship with the hikers. They want to feel like they're a part of the crew and not just a means of hauling gear. So it's important to feed the relationship by never overworking them. They'll never forget who over-packed them or who asked them to carry their load for too long, and the relationship will be bruised forever.

Bringing Wilson and Bert into our lives proved to be a tremendously fulfilling experience. Working with them, taking them on hikes, and having them around was truly a dream realized for me, so much so that my wife and I would add to the pack goat total on our land as more time passed.

We now have eight pack goats, and the animals are simply a joy to have around. Perhaps the most impressive of the bunch is Floyd, of the LaMancha breed, with no horns and cute, little tulip ears, features that would make him look smaller than other pack goats. But the fact is that he is smaller, significantly smaller, than most other pack goats. For some reason, Floyd never grew to the size we expected him to be. That, combined with his lack of horns and those tiny ears, makes him look positively diminutive. My wife and I were worried about Floyd and his ability to keep up on the trail and his ability to carry a load, his ability to be part of the team.

"No problem," Floyd would say if he could talk. And he'd say it with a smile.

What a joy this little goat has turned out to be! He takes on a full load based on his weight and is basically attached to my hip wherever we go together, whether it's hiking in the backcountry or walking around the property. He's at the top of the pecking order among our goats, and they all know where Floyd's place is when we're on the trail. Floyd is fun in so many ways—he's intelligent enough to open gate latches that are not properly secured with tight springs—and he follows me around like a shadow with his little undersized pack on his back, displaying a servant's heart at all times.

That's right! Floyd absolutely has a servant's heart. But his many positive attributes would be overshadowed if he didn't display the most important attribute that any pack goat or salesperson or athlete or actor can have.

Floyd has a work ethic.

A servant's heart is a powerful thing to bring to your life and your work. But it can't stand alone. A servant's heart needs to be teamed with a work ethic that can never be questioned by bosses, suppliers, customers…

Or the person in the mirror.

CHAPTER 14

A HARD-WORKING WORK ETHIC

love my work. I enjoy being a professional. I take great pride in it. I look forward to meeting with and helping dairy producers keep their cows healthy so they can get the most out of them. I love the process of joining the cows in the pen, of interacting with these tremendous creatures, of making sure they're better off when I leave a producer's farm than they were when I got there.

But as much as I love my work, I do not live to work.

I work to live.

That can't be said enough.

There are several not-very-subtle differences regarding these two concepts. Some people, for instance, really do live for their work because they love what they do so much. It's not an unhealthy thing for them because what they do feeds their souls and fulfills them. An artist would be a perfect example. But far too many other people spend their waking hours at a job that simply grinds them down, a job that comes with few rewards outside of a paycheck. Then there are people who work to live. Young people just out of school—with no money in the bank and maybe a student loan on the other side of the ledger—starting their careers may believe they work to live. It's probably more accurate to say, "They have to work just to live."

Then there's me. I work so that I can live the life I love in the mountains of Southern Colorado, traveling to great hiking spots and national parks with family, friends, and our pack goats. I'm fortunate that I have earned quite a bit of control over my schedule, often spending the workday in our home office that has views of the spectacular Sangre de Cristo Mountains. I can hike in the mornings and evenings and spend plenty of time with my wife as well as our animals. I can schedule my sales calls so that I'm gone for just a solid block of time, usually a very full week every month that finds me on the road, meeting with dairy producers and constantly learning about how I can best help them.

It's a nice life; it's the life for which I've always strived.

If you're a lawyer who passed the bar exam in Delaware, chances are pretty good that you're going to be a lawyer in Delaware for the rest of your professional career. Unless you change your career path and maybe take a job in sales. If you're in sales you could be in surfboard sales in California, lobster sales in Maine, or pecan sales in South Carolina. Sales is the most mobile career there is, whether the mobility is geographic or from one industry to another. I know a successful wine salesman in Minneapolis who went into software sales and didn't miss a beat. He's a guy who'd started his sales career selling fine material to clothing manufacturers. The fact that you're in sales means that you have a lot of options regarding what you sell and where you do it. Make sure you use those options for the purpose of living a life that completely fulfills you. Not many people in other professions have such an opportunity.

It's probably more accurate to say it's a nice reward, a reward for years of hard work and being honest with myself about my work ethic.

What is a work ethic? How can it be measured? There's no scale to gauge it in anyone. A work ethic may mean something different from one person to another. I recall being impressed by a co-worker when I was starting my sales career in Montana. He appeared to always be busy. He logged more days on the road and more nights in hotels than anyone else on our staff. When he was in the office he was on the phone with ranchers and suppliers. He was always letting the rest of the sales force know that he was setting up meetings here and there before turning in his expense report. The guy was absolutely a flurry of activity. He had a work ethic.

He also had very little success.

Many people confuse action with progress, motion with output. It's a terrible mistake that far too many people in all professions make. I came to a true understanding about my work ethic shortly after I discovered my servant's heart: I realized that discovering my servant's heart was what opened the door for me to sift through the difference between working hard and having a good work ethic.

I realized then that my former co-worker in Montana did not actually have a work ethic. He may not have even worked hard, but rather kept up the appearance that he was always in motion and, thereby, making progress.

A recent study concluded that the aggregate of the American workforce uses only 54% of our paid time off every year.[3] Why is that? Many people who are a part of our workforce say it's because they're simply so busy. With all the demands of their jobs, they don't have time to take a beach vacation on the Jersey Shore or visit The Great Wall of China. They don't even have time for a weekend getaway at a B&B an hour away from home. They need to work. More to the point: they need to be seen working. They need to be seen working so that others think they're working hard. They need to make their superiors believe they work hard. They need to make their direct reports feel the same way. How else are those subordinates going to learn about hard work?

Americans work hard, and that's nothing for which to apologize. I work hard.

> "There is no substitute for hard work."
> —*Thomas A. Edison*

More important, I work smart.

In our culture we have a long and mistaken belief that "hours spent working" means "hours being productive." It's understandable, given the fact that many people are paid an hourly wage and our history of unionized production lines allows management to assign a number of widgets produced for any number of hours worked by a single person or the collective hours worked by a crew.

Thomas Edison may have touted the benefits of "hard work," but it's probably more accurate to say the inventor of the incandescent light bulb—and so many other items that changed the world—had a tremendous work ethic. The perfect example of his work ethic was reflected in his response to a person asking if he had failed in making a light bulb work after trying 10,000 different times. "I have not failed," Edison responded. "I've just found 10,000 ways that won't work."[4] He knew what he wanted to get done, and he looked upon "failures" as part of the road he traveled to get done what he wanted to get done.

That's a work ethic.

When I'm working, I'm working. I'm not listening to music, I'm not forwarding funny e-mails to friends, I'm not looking out at the mountains and wishing I were leading the goats on a hike. I'm working. That's the fundamental difference between working hard and exhibiting a work ethic. Whether I'm at my desk for an hour cleaning up some paperwork or I'm there for six hours making phone calls to producers and suppliers, I'm working. I'm making sure that progress is made based on the progress that needs to be made, not based on the number of hours I spend at my desk.

I like to say, "The job is the boss." That saying is what motivates me to work hard, do my job well, and always know that "the job" may be "the boss," but "the job" is not "the life" that I lead. "The job" is the means by which I have built the life I lead.

I do not work for money. Money comes because I perform my job well. It's almost a by-product. The thought of fattening my wallet is not the thing that motivates me when I'm meeting a customer. Other thoughts motivate me to do a great job at selling, other thoughts encourage me to tap in to the work ethic I've developed.

What motivates you? What is the thing that makes you want to work hard? It's okay to say money; we all need to eat. But once you push back from the table, what is it that you can do with the money you earn in sales that motivates you? Is it that you're able to give to a charity that's important to you? Is it that you want to provide for your family? Is it that you wish to take your family to ski the legendary powder of Niseko, Japan, where the resort gets twice as much snow as North American resorts get?

Millions of Americans work hard every day, come home pooped, refuse to use half of their vacation days, and spend New Year's Eve wondering where the year went and why they keep waking up in the middle of the night thinking about work.

Conversely, developing the right work ethic propels a person. It may take an hour or it may take all week, but getting a project to the finish line as efficiently as possible is generally the best way to judge someone's work ethic, including your own.

Bringing it all home for the sales professional, the rewards you can reap when you combine a servant's heart with a strong work ethic are legion. A commitment to combine the two and bring them forth as you go on sales calls and serve your customers will bring you fulfillment and a sense of purpose that will allow you to experience the true definition of success. In every way imaginable, you'll find abundance showing up in your life—from financial success to meaningful relationships to satisfaction with the direction of your life. Since I began combining my own servant's heart with a work ethic that's as honest as it can be, I have experienced abundance in all areas of my life. The great reality here is that this abundance and feeling of success is available to anyone who embraces and lives by these principles. It's available to you, if you simply make the choices that allow it to happen.

Floyd, the dimunitive pack goat with the outsized work ethic

Which brings me back to Floyd and the reason why that little pack goat holds such a special place in my heart. Floyd is as hardy as any animal I've ever encountered. He loves his life roaming about our acreage, foraging, walking around with our donkey—named Donkey Hodie—and climbing the rocks with his fellow goats. This herd is never without the protection of our two Great Pyrenees dogs, Luna and Baxter, and the whole crew is happy and healthy on a great stretch of land.

All of that is good. Our property provides a great setup for the goats and the land because the land offers room and food for the goats while the animals' presence improves the quality of the land. It's a great example of wonderful salesperson/customer relationship: both sides giving and receiving.

When I put the specially engineered Floyd-sized pack on that little goat's back, loaded up with supplies, he displays a work ethic that is impossible to quantify. He's right there at my hip no matter where we go or how far we go. He never "squawks" or complains; he just goes and goes and goes and does so with a friendly spirit that shines like a halo above his head.

It's impossible to say that Floyd works hard because he knows that he's living the goat's equivalent of the "Life of Riley" on our land. But it's entirely possible to know that the way he works is a reflection of an animal who was born with a very admirable work ethic that teams perfectly with his servant's heart.

> Could you sell ice cubes to an Eskimo? If you said yes, you probably believe you have a "salesman's personality." Or is the "salesman's personality" just some silly stereotype we've developed as a society? I submit that there are as many personalities in sales as there are salespeople.

Every person is different, so every salesperson is different. Embrace that. I know of many people in dairy sales who once worked on their family farms, for instance, and wanted to stay connected to the dairy business. They're not fast talkers, they're not slick in any way, but they have tremendous experience in the industry, and that allows them to connect with their customers and deliver the necessary answers and products. A servant's heart and strong work ethic will enable anyone to be successful in sales, regardless of personality type.

CHAPTER 15

YOU'RE NEVER WORKING FOR NOTHING

n my market there are farms and farmers with whom I do not wish to do business. Ever since I started my career in sales, I have wanted to work only with the best, most reputable, most progressive customers I can. From Montana to Florida to my present position, I have made the extra effort to work with top-end producers, people who can be a good fit for me as well as the suppliers whose product I sell. I have always aimed to align myself with people who are the best at what they do.

Why is that?

My goal is always to deal with producers who are as passionate about their work as I am about mine, producers to whom I can proudly point when speaking with a prospect and say: "This is the type of dairy I work with every day." I want the prospect to know that I consider his dairy operation to be among the best in the business.

I do not aim to build up volume for the sake of building up volume, to work with every single dairy doing business in New Mexico and West Texas. That may sound strange; after all, doesn't a salesperson want to sell all he or she can? Yes, some salespeople do aim to sell, sell, sell, but that's not me. I want to help the best dairy producers become even better.

> Working with a dairy that does business the right way reflects right back on my own reputation as well as my self-regard. I appreciate that the relationship says something about the quality of work I do.

My customer Ben is a wonderful man who has been in the New Mexico dairy business his whole life. He grew up on a dairy, learned the proverbial ropes of the business as a kid, went away to school for the dual purpose of playing college football and getting a degree in agricultural business, and, a few years later, was completely in charge of a dairy ten miles from where he grew up. By the time he was 30, he owned two major dairies right down the road from each other. He's a pro's pro: he knows everything that's happening and everything that's supposed to happen every day on a dairy farm.

When I was first getting into dairy nutrition sales, I was impressed from afar with Ben. Everyone I talked to referred to him with a certain amount of reverence, as a gentleman who really knows his stuff, treats his employees well, engenders loyalty from them, and runs a first-class operation.

Being aligned with Ben, I believed, would be a real plus.

So, while I was developing business in the area, I called Ben's dairy and spoke with his wife, Justine. She was (and is) a very sweet, friendly lady who didn't hesitate to tell me when and where I could get in touch with Ben. Once I connected with him, I realized that they were both very genuine, wonderful people who were happy to sit down and talk to me about the dairy they operate, introduce me to people who work there, and show me some of the things that make the whole operation so successful. There was nothing egotistical or phony about them, and I really liked that as we shared stories about our backgrounds, our travels, and our families.

Shortly after I got to know Ben, I asked if he'd like to look at a proposal. I wanted to get his reaction to what my company and I could do to help him realize even better production on the dairy. He said that would be fine and gave me all his rations, his pricing, his restrictions—minimum and maximum feeding levels on certain ingredients—and was extremely open about so many of the things that had made his dairy such a success.

It was voluminous information he offered, and I was grateful for the opportunity. I retreated to my office, did some work with the data he'd provided, and realized there were a few opportunities that I thought were significant. After putting together a detailed proposal, I printed out a number of pages with my findings, placed them all in a nice, professionally prepared packet, and returned to Ben's dairy.

"I like what you have to say," Ben said as he perused the binder following my presentation. He'd brought me to his office and respectfully listened to all I'd had to tell him. He asked a few very insightful questions that I was able to answer pretty quickly and assuredly. "Very interesting," he said more than once while nodding his head during my answers.

"So, what do you think?" I inquired. "Could this sort of thing be a benefit to your operation?"

"You've done a great job on your proposal, Clancy," Ben replied as he looked down at the material. "It's full of interesting stuff and…I'm gonna give it some thought."

After I left his dairy, I felt very good about myself, sure that I'd conducted myself well and that I'd given Ben a bit of information that could really help him optimize things. But when the following weeks went by and I didn't hear from him, I figured that was it: I'd stepped up to the plate and I'd gotten a hit…but it wasn't a home run.

I continued showing up at his dairy while I made my rounds in the area—just to stay in touch. I never brought up the proposal when I saw Ben, though I did bring him articles and any other information I thought he'd find interesting. We roamed around the pens together a number of times in the ensuing months and wound up having some really great conversations about his business. That was when I suggested I help a little around his dairy. I was in the area every other week anyway, and it would be a pleasure to help out such a wonderful man and his family.

I showed up and busied myself around Ben's dairy whenever I was in the area, and everyone there was always pleasant. But since Ben never said anything more about my proposal, I wondered if our relationship was just sort of stuck in neutral. "Should I ask him if I should make another proposal?" I mused. But after mulling our conversations over, I realized that, clearly, he wasn't ready to make a switch to a new nutritionist. He'd been with his present nutritionist for more than 20 years, and the two of them had developed a very close personal and professional relationship.

I had to respect that.

If all the dairies in West Texas and eastern New Mexico were in the same state, that state would be the third or fourth biggest milk producer in the U.S. It's huge business, and approximately 60% of the money a producer invests every year goes into feed. As such, no producer is going to make a snap decision to change or tell me he'll sample what I have to offer for a few months and let me know what he thinks. Every sales business has its own pace of development and, with it, its own selling cycle. In the dairy nutrition business, our selling cycle is exceptionally long. It's vital for a salesperson to know this pace and work within its limits in order to optimize results for all involved. If you try to "push the river" you will likely wind up making costly mistakes that will slow sales growth while also damaging your reputation and that of your company. I always say, "It's better to go right than fast," and that motto has helped me build my reputation in the marketplace and build lasting sales relationships.

That said, I had identified a few things on his farm that could use a little supervision. I asked Ben if I could evaluate some of the forage on the farm as well as a few other odd jobs. "I'll come by on my regular rounds and spend the same amount of time as I do with my current customers," I told Ben. "Then I'll be able to furnish you with some information you may not currently be getting."

Ben agreed to that, and I started coming to his dairy with my Penn State shaker box that separates the different particles of the feed ingredients within the Total Mixed Rations (TMR). Getting the TMR right is vital to helping the cow digest the feeds properly, making sure she does not sort the ration and eat only what she wants. Proper TMR also promotes the health of the rumen and ensures that there's proper fiber mass for the microorganisms to live in.

So, I began shaking out Ben's rations every time I was down in his area. As a result of what we learned, we made a few adjustments in how things were being done at the dairy's feed center, and that resulted in many pounds of extra milk being produced and headed to market. As my work was yielding results, I got the feeling that Ben really appreciated having me around, that he was finding significant value in my collaboration with his team.

The Penn State shaker box is easy to use. I just shake it, rotate it, shake it again, and then weigh the feed that has fallen through the various-sized holes on the three shelves inside the box. By evaluating these numbers, I can determine what's called the physical properties of the ration. Making sure the percentages of feed on each shelf are correct helps a cow make the most milk from the feed she eats.

I continued traveling to Ben's dairy every few weeks and going about my duties, rain or shine, summer or winter, on windy days and even the occasional snowy day on the New Mexico plains for which no man or beast is ever ready. I received no recompense, but that was fine: I was doing the work because I knew what I was doing was helping a good person's dairy production. Sometimes when the weather was bad, Ben or Justine would call me and tell me I didn't need to come by, but I stayed true to my commitment. After all, if the work I was doing was important enough to do on beautiful days, it was important enough to do on days when the weather made it more of a challenge.

After several months of doing this work, Ben pulled me aside and mentioned that he'd like to bring me onto his payroll as a consultant. "No," I responded. "I don't care to do that. The day you pay me anything is the day I become your dairy's nutritionist." I told him I was impressed by his dairy, I was happy to be there, and I was learning a lot—so it really was a mutually beneficial relationship. What he wanted to do, obviously, was have his cake and eat it too: paying me as a consultant while keeping his relationship with his longtime nutritionist. But if I'd agreed to that sort of a setup, I'd be stuck in that role forever.

In all, I worked for Ben gratis for about 18 months and, time and time again, he would tell me he was really interested and impressed with what my team and I were doing at his dairy. He never let me think that I wasn't appreciated there or that I wasn't adding tremendous value to his operation. The problem, he told me one day, was: "Clancy…I'm just a really loyal guy. But the good news for you eventually is…I'm a really loyal guy."

He didn't have to say that. I recognized it.

These dairies in West Texas and New Mexico have an amazing number of moving parts, things that can go wrong, things that need to go right, things that are vital for the dairy to be a successful operation, and Ben had his finger on the pulse of every single part of his business. He didn't make any decision in haste.

The feeling I got was that Ben wanted to make a change; he probably felt like turning his dairy nutrition needs over to me would be beneficial for his dairy. But he needed to examine such a move from every conceivable angle. That's why, right around Thanksgiving a few years ago, Ben told me he wanted to speak to me as I arrived at his dairy. "Go ahead and do your rounds," he waved his arm toward the cow pens. "Then come find me before you leave."

As the early winter sun was hurrying toward the western horizon in late afternoon, I finished up my work and found Ben in his office. "You wanted to see me before I go," I said.

"Yes, Clancy…" Ben said slowly as he put down some papers and removed his glasses. "I'm ready to make a change," he said matter-of-factly. He'd go on to say that he was going to turn over the nutrition business for one dairy to me while keeping his present nutritionist at his other dairy. "I want to avail myself of what you do," he reported before telling me that he'd have a conversation with his present nutritionist over the holidays regarding the new arrangement.

"What can I do to earn your business?" You've heard that question asked. You very likely may have asked it yourself. It's a question that rings hollow to most prospects because what they often interpret that statement to mean is: "What can I do right here and right now to get you to buy my product or service and, thereby, separate yourself from your money?" I suggest you never ask, "What can I do to earn your business?" Instead, figure out for yourself what you can do to make what you offer something that your prospect will find invaluable. Do whatever it takes to show your prospect how you can help, and allow your prospect to make the decision to become your customer. That's the difference between selling and *Selling by Serving.*

It was a perfect example of infinite patience yielding results: I spent a great deal of time offering up my services to Ben, and then, one day, he suddenly turned over a significant piece of business to me. He had made the decision when *he was ready.*

Since then Ben, Justine, and I have developed a tremendous relationship. We've achieved things on that dairy that Ben has admitted he didn't think were possible. In the process, we've become very close professionally and personally. It's been a special relationship that has paid off in so many ways.

I'm convinced that I was right not to push at all during that year-and-a-half period I worked for free on his dairy. Sure, I might have gotten him to hire me if I'd nudged a little bit, but I knew I had to give Ben room and time. I offered myself to him, and he'd given me a chance to show I could make a difference. He'd needed to put a lot of thought into the situation, and I was smart to let him do that. As such, when it came time for him to turn his dairy nutrition over to me, he was fully convinced that he was making the right decision. There would be no staying awake at night wondering if he'd made a mistake, no second-guessing with Justine over coffee in the morning. He'd seen me work, and he was aware of the many ways I could help him boost production. Ben knew he could count on me, so when he made the decision, he was comfortable doing so.

That's what everyone in sales should want: a customer who is totally committed to the product, the service, and the relationship that is being offered. We call that loyalty, and the value of loyalty in the world of sales is beyond measure.

CHAPTER 16

A SERVANT'S HEART
ON FOUR PAWS

He gave and gave and gave. He gave, literally, until he didn't have anything left to give.

I would never say my Border Collie Griff was my favorite dog ever. Dog lovers simply do not measure their dogs that way. Dog trainers like I used to be do not think of dogs that way either. Each dog is different and special, each dog has a personality that is uniquely his or her own, and each dog connects with different people in different ways. A working dog like a Border Collie needs to connect with his or her owner—when the two are in sync, it's a wonderful relationship in the field and at home.

> A Border Collie whose coat is predominantly white is not a good dog to have in the pasture. That's because the sheep will think it's another sheep and won't react the same way they do when they're being herded by a dog who sports a darker coat.

I guess it makes sense to think that Griff and I were destined for each other; after all, it was an act of friendship and a handshake deal one day that ensured I'd take home a dog in the future.

That dog turned out to be Griff.

The genesis of my life with Griff resulted from my friend Jeff losing his own dog. The dog had run away, which is not too common, but it does happen sometimes with working dogs. Jeff needed a dog to help him tend to his sheep, but he didn't have much money. I sold him my Border Collie named Megan because he was in a bind, but it wasn't without a little trepidation because I'd been offered quite a bit of money by other people wanting to purchase Megan. Regardless, Jeff and I made a deal that I would get a pick from Megan's litter of puppies in the not too distant future.

In fairly short order, we found a terrific male dog to mate with Megan, and she gave birth to a litter of five. Four of the puppies had markings that reflected Megan's black-and-white coat, but one little guy sported a rare red coat all over his body.

> A sheep dog's job is to dominate herd animals and intimidate them like he's hunting them. The dog may be smaller, but the dog's agility, attitude, and intelligence means he can herd 300-pound rams in the morning—animals who are trying to attack him with their horns—and then spend the afternoon nudging a lamb forward with his nose so that the lamb is never too far away from the mother.

When breeding Border Collies, it's important that the dogs are not bred for color but rather their ability to work. It doesn't matter if one of these dogs has feet that don't point perfectly straight or displays a questionable posture. They are not bred for the Westminster Dog Show; they are bred to run and run and run, herding and reacting to their masters' commands. That's not to say Border Collies aren't beautiful animals. They are. But their athleticism and herding instincts are what breeders try to maximize when breeding.

I trained Griff, and two others from the same litter, to herd sheep. I sold the other two after they'd gotten a great start on their training, but Griff was my dog, and he took to my training like a fish to water. He followed commands so quickly and readily, it was like he and I were thinking with the same brain. It's important to know that working dogs like Griff work for the chance to work some more—they've been bred for centuries to work in any kind of weather conditions during any time of year. All they really require at the end of a day in the field is maybe a gentle pat on the head and definitely hearing their master saying nothing more than, "That'll do." That's when they know it's time to shift into a lower gear and look forward to the next day of work. They don't require big hugs and aggressive rubs behind the ears to know they're appreciated: "That'll do" and the promise of working again the next day do just fine.

Griff was everything a sheepherder would want in a Border Collie. His enthusiasm and intelligence were unsurpassed, and he won the Montana State Sheep Dog Trials as a yearling. I was in the perfect place then for a special dog like Griff. I was herding sheep all day every day, and this wonderful dog was omnipresent in my life. Unlike any other dogs I had at the time, Griff would stay inside with me instead of out in the kennel, but that hardly meant he was pampered. It could be a cold, rainy morning, and he would wake up before sunrise ready to work. He would hop into the truck and never make a peep about how far away from home we were going or how long his workday was. Through snowstorms and long days under the hot summer sun he would work. That little guy would make the sheep look like they were moving in slow motion as he ran alongside them and kept them together—he was just lightning fast. I saw him run over 100 miles in a day more than a few times, and he'd never hold back on effort during the workday or on affection when the workday was done.

> **"If you want something done, ask a busy person to do it."**
> —*Lucille Ball*

Griff's workdays couldn't last forever, though. Like all great athletes, Griff began to slow down as the rigors of time and years of hard work took their collective toll on him. As such, I lightened Griff's workload and one morning took him out to a relatively tiny pasture where I kept a small flock of sheep. I gave Griff the command to gather the sheep and he set out right away, excited for the action and anxious for the feeling of accomplishment he'd earned so many times before.

But he couldn't outrun the sheep; his body simply could not carry him fast enough anymore. I couldn't bear to see him having so much trouble, and, as always, Griff seemed to be thinking right along with me. He ceased running, stopped trying in vain to herd the sheep, and finished his working career right then and there. He sat down, turned his head toward me and away from the sheep—something he'd never done before as he'd always looked at me from the other side of a herd, making sure his flock was always under his gaze. He gave me an expression that could not be understood as saying anything other than, "That's all, Boss."

Griff retired that day looking like he wanted to cry, and yet he also looked somehow content with his lifetime of dedicated service. I shed a tear for him as I look back, feeling a mix of emotions that words cannot convey. Never again would he be out in the pasture, herding sheep. Never again would he hear me bark commands and react as if he was thinking the same thing. But he would hear me give him one more command. "That'll do," I said to Griff as I accepted his retirement. It wasn't a "that'll do" that he'd heard over the past dozen years after a hard day's work; no, it was a "that'll do" that thanked him for all the work he'd put in for me over the years.

I would do everything I could to help Griff enjoy his "retirement." He went on to enjoy lazy days around the house, long naps in the sunshine or before the fireplace, and leisurely walks to the river where he'd watch me cast for trout. I'll never forget how animated Griff would get when I got a bite and started reeling in a fish—it was like he felt the excitement as much as I did.

It would be difficult to say goodbye to Griff three years later, but I remember the lessons he taught me, and I carry them with me every day. The joy he found in his work inspires me to find the same joy in mine. The servant's heart he brought to me is the same servant's heart I try every day to bring to my customers. He taught me to be selfless, to be humble, to work hard and enjoy doing so, and to savor the rewards of doing a job well for someone who needs a job done well.

Griff, my companion, work partner, and teacher

> "The effect you have on others is the most valuable
> currency there is."   —*Jim Carrey*

By being the dog that he was, Griff was so memorable for me. When I think about him to this day, I realize how important he was in teaching me that work in itself can be and should be a reward, that fulfillment lives in the satisfaction of helping others. Having that feeling at the end of a workday is what I strive to have, knowing that reaching sales goals and pocketing material rewards fall out of realizing that satisfaction.

It is not the other way around. Find satisfaction and fulfillment in the work, and the rewards will be derived from that.

My great good fortune in having Griff share his life with me is that I saw the servant's heart in action before I ever entertained a career in sales. The effect he had on me was so profound, however, that he has had a special place in my heart all these years—and all these animals—later.

CHAPTER 17

YOUR CUSTOMER
IS YOUR GUEST

Having material blessings is nice. Sharing material blessings is much, much better.

My wife and I—along with the dogs and the goats—live in a truly unique place in south-central Colorado, surrounded by the famed Sangre de Cristo Mountain Range. The Sangre de Cristo Mountains were named by a Spanish explorer, a man who witnessed the sunrise on the red-tinted snowy peaks all around him and declared: "Sangre de Cristo." The phrase translates into "Blood of Christ," and the vistas afforded by these mountains never get old, especially as seasons change and different colors are featured and accented on the landscape.

A number of Colorado's famed "14ers"—mountains whose peaks climb more than 14,000 feet above sea level—make up parts of this mountain range, one that draws painters, photographers, hikers, mountain bikers, and sightseers from around the world. There's Blanca Peak, standing 14,345 feet high, Crestone Peak just 51 feet lower, Kit Carson Peak at 14, 165 feet high, and so many others. It's a spectacular sight, no matter what the season.

But the peak that has drawn my interest and my attention the most during the years we've lived here is Dreamy Mountain. Dreamy

Mountain is not a 14er, not even close. It's a relatively small, uneven pyramid of rocks set in a valley just a short hike from our house.

I venture out to Dreamy Mountain just about every day when I'm home, the place we've happily christened "Goat Camp." Heading to the mountain and back provides a vigorous hike, and climbing to the top of Dreamy Mountain pays off in so many ways, as well. The 360-degree views are priceless, and the goats are able to climb the steep, rocky terrain with grace and ease that never ceases to amaze me—these animals are truly in their element on Dreamy Mountain.

Whether the sun is rising in the east and highlighting the red hue of the Sangre de Cristo Mountains or setting in the west, bathing the valley in light and long shadows, the top of Dreamy Mountain is a truly special place any time of year.

Dreamy Mountain

There is no one path to the top of Dreamy Mountain. There is no trail, and there are no signs showing the way. There's only instinct, experience, and the method we all use of learning so many things in our lives: trial and error. I have spent a great deal of time climbing up the west side, the east side, the north side. I've traversed and made minimal progress. I've found myself stuck and needing to retreat with the goats hopping all around me like dancers in a ballet.

None of these difficult trips up Dreamy Mountain would I ever consider a waste of time, however, as I was able to learn with every step whether I found purchase on a particular rock or lost a foothold and wound up with a bruise as a result. Every trip up was a learning experience to the point that I kept in mind that famous Thomas Edison quote about light bulbs—"I have not failed; I've just found 10,000 ways that won't work."[5]—each time I approached the mountain. Finally, after many tries, I determined the exact right and least difficult way to climb up, bask in the view, and feel the sense of accomplishment that comes with overcoming a challenge.

But what good is enjoying something if you can't also share it? Since the first day I scanned the horizon from the top of Dreamy Mountain, I've been determined to share the view and the experience with others. My wife often joins the goats and me on climbs to the top, and sometimes friends who live near us will join us for an afternoon.

What I really like, however, is when a friend, work colleague, or customer comes to visit. It's really fun having someone come see how we live, enjoy the house and the views, and engage in good, long conversations about any number of subjects. But what I know makes just about everyone's visit truly unique and special is when we all get up in the morning and put on the hiking gear. I encourage guests to wear a pair of good, light athletic shoes or boots as well as loose-fitting pants or shorts and a shirt that can afford them plenty of movement. A fair amount of sunscreen is also recommended.

> "Your abundance is not measured by what you have; it is created by what you share."
> —Heidi Catherine Culbertson, author of Wisdom and Recipes: Things I Would Have Shared with My Daughter

As host and tour guide, I wear all that and more. My wide-brimmed hiking cap keeps the hot sun off my face, and my daypack with extra clothes, rain gear, a first aid kit, an emergency whistle, and, finally, a can of bear spray is a must. Dangerous interactions with Colorado wildlife are extremely rare, but I'd never stray too far from Goat Camp without being prepared for any possibility. As I often say, "Better to have it and not need it than need it and not have it."

When my guests and I take off for Dreamy Mountain with a few of the goats alongside, I embrace the feeling of adventure but also the joy of sharing. Sharing the Dreamy Mountain experience with anyone is a special feeling, and I can't deny that it is extremely reminiscent of helping a client through the buying process. That's because I truly see myself as the leader in both instances, the person providing direction to another person and helping that person achieve something that he or she would not be able to capture alone.

There are differences, of course. My customers generally hire me for my dairy nutrition knowledge as well as the rations I provide in order to help their farms work at the highest possible level. What I bring to their businesses is an existential necessity for their farms. A trip to the top of Dreamy Mountain with the goats is merely an elective, something that people are usually anxious to do when I tell them what an enjoyable experience it's going to be.

Now, one could say that I "sell" my guests on a hike to the top of Dreamy Mountain. But I disagree. I lead, and I do so the same way I lead people through the buying process. I know from experience that one of our guests is not going to make it to the top of Dreamy Mountain without my showing the way, just as I know my customers depend on my expertise to guide them to the right nutrition for their dairy cows.

When my guests and I get to the base of Dreamy Mountain, we usually stop and enjoy a drink of water. I also make sure I give the goats plenty of water before the climb. That's also when I "check in" with my guest—when they're looking up at this pile of rocks, they're getting a different perspective than they have looking at it from Goat Camp. "Are you sure you want to do this?" "Will you feel comfortable on these rocks?" "We'll go up there at your pace, okay?"

That last question is very important, and it's vital that I phrase it and deliver it in a reassuring fashion. Some guests are hesitant while others are anxious to start the climb. But not a single guest has retreated at this point, and I believe it's because they all know that I am sincere and committed to guiding them.

When it comes to sales, your customer knows you're a salesperson. You don't need to show it. What you need to display is the sincerity and authenticity you display naturally when dealing with a customer. What you're doing is guiding your customer, helping him discover something for himself.

Last summer I had a colleague named Steve at Goat Camp for an evening. Shortly after he arrived, he and I walked the acreage with our eight goats, donkey, and two Great Pyrenees dogs—Luna and Baxter. About midway through the tour, I pointed at Dreamy Mountain and asked, "Would you like to take some of the goats and climb to the top tomorrow morning?"

"Sure," Steve answered with a willingness that told me the next day's hike would be a lot of fun.

Off we went the following morning, before it got too hot. The sky was blue, and many of the mountaintops displayed considerable accents of snow even though it was mid-summer. Steve, an avid skier, joked that he should have brought his skis with him and hiked up to the snow for a run. I mentioned that he must really love skiing to consider hiking to the top of a 14er wearing ski boots and carrying skis just to get a single run in.

Steve laughed: "Ha! Just joking. That's what chair lifts are for."

The two of us hiked along with four goats—Floyd, Zeppy, Sherman, and Wilson—and rested at the base of Dreamy Mountain, enjoying some water and conversation. It was there that I advised Steve one last time about the path to the top, what to look out for, how the goats would behave during the climb, and everything he could expect as we made our way up. Then I assured him one last time that we'd be going at his pace.

His pace was pretty good, so he followed my line and listened to my direction, and we were at the top in short order. Steve was enthralled by the way the goats climbed gracefully to the top and then bounced around once the climb was over. We gave the goats a few treats and talked a bit about the vistas that surrounded us, as well as a little about business. Then Steve noticed that three of the goats were staring at something in the brush below that had gotten their attention. The goats were still, their tails stuck out straight, their eyes did not blink.

Was it a bear? A mountain lion? Both animals are indigenous to the area, but it's not too often that they show themselves.

We both concentrated on where the goats were looking and couldn't identify anything. Then we scanned the valley below for movement, a tree or a bush that was being rustled by an animal. But nothing was apparent. After a couple minutes of concentrating on what was holding the goats' attention, Steve spoke up. "Look right down there…" he said slowly as he pointed. "There's an easel with a canvas on it. See that?" Indeed, someone wearing a big hat had come out to capture the early morning sunshine and paint a landscape.

There's always something new to see from atop Dreamy Mountain.

Hiking with the goats, climbing with them, and watching their reaction to the painter provided a real "aha!" experience for Steve. He'd arrived with no real preconceptions about the goats other than that he knew—and was thrilled—that they were nothing like cats. "They're really a lot like dogs," he told me over lunch that day at Goat Camp. "And that's a big-time compliment."

Guiding Steve or anyone else to the top of Dreamy Mountain is vastly different than the hard-charging salesperson racing to the top for his or her own gain, leaving the customer to struggle and question whether the buying decision he or she is making is right. In such a situation, the customer may decide to "turn around and head back down," meaning he or she chooses not to reach the top (i.e., complete the sales process). Even if a sale does happen, the customer may conclude that the "guide"—the salesperson—is more concerned with making the sale than with the customer's welfare. If that's the case, will the customer be taking any more excursions (doing any more business) with that individual?

Considering your prospects or customers, it's helpful to think of your role not as a salesperson, but as a guide. You are helping your customer through the sales process, just as you would help that person climb a mountain. You check in with that person as you begin the journey together, making sure you're both ready to embark and have everything the two of you need, including confidence that the leader—you—has the customer's best interests at heart.

The process means that you provide helpful information along the way that will make the trip more comfortable, interesting, and valuable. You continually make sure the customer doesn't have any hesitations about continuing upward. You provide the confidence.

By approaching the process this way, you will ensure that you and your customer reach the top together. Both of you reach your goal at the same time, and you are equally rewarded for the effort you've made together. As a result, your customer will likely be willing to go anywhere with you as his or her guide.

Now, I don't know if I'd call Steve old-fashioned. But he does engage in the old-fashioned practice of writing letters, addressing envelopes, putting stamps on them, and dropping them into the mail. So, I wasn't surprised a few days after his visit when a letter arrived thanking us for the stay and raving about the trip to the top of Dreamy Mountain. He'd been showing pictures to family and friends and telling everyone about the great time he'd had at Goat Camp.

Receiving his note was really gratifying, and I nodded as I put the letter down. I had provided Steve with an experience that was truly unique for him. I'd prepared him for the trip up Dreamy Mountain and then led him every step of the way. He would not have done that alone, nor would he have done it with four goats dancing all around him or reacting to the painter in our midst. His pictures and memories will last a long time.

I always strive to lead my guests and customers, making sure they're comfortable in the endeavor and grateful for my guidance. Keeping that in mind helps me to not necessarily "make the sale" or "climb the mountain" for some self-serving purpose.

Rather, that mindset helps me to perform all my duties with a servant's heart.

CHAPTER 18

OVERCOMING THE GOOD OL' BOYS' NETWORK

I can't say it enough: there is no "salesman's" personality. Salespeople are not all fast talkers trying to pull the wool over a customer's eyes. Salespeople are not clad in clothing made up of so much synthetic material that they're a walking fire hazard. Salespeople are not anything like they've often been portrayed in movies and television shows. Each salesperson is different from the next salesperson and the next salesperson and the next salesperson. Some are tall, some are short, some are talkers, some are not—each one is different.

But there is one thing that some salespeople are and on which they rely heavily to get results: They're members of the Good Ol' Boys' Network.

There's no secret as to what the Good Ol' Boys' Network is. It's endemic to just about every business. Advertising agencies, brokerage houses, insurance company offices have traditionally been bastions of the Good Ol' Boys' Network, where people are hired for a position almost entirely because they know someone or are married to the daughter of some high-up.

The Good Ol' Boys' Network exists in sales, as well. I realized that when I got into sales in Montana, but I really came face to face with the Good Ol' Boys' Network when I got to Florida.

Now, I may be a mountain man, a long-time resident of the American West who loves nothing more than living in and hiking around the undisputed majesty of the Rocky Mountains. But I loved my time in Florida and treasured the years I spent there.

I really took a professional chance when I got there. I had built up a pretty good business in Montana, and it was hard to step away from it. But circumstances being what they were, I headed to Florida and began looking for a new job in sales.

There were more than a few barriers to be faced down when I got to the Sunshine State: I was in my 40s, I was in a new place, and I knew absolutely no one. But I also knew Florida was an economic power-house—the state's economy is the 17th largest in the world[6]—and I figured there would be opportunities for me once I got there. I didn't see myself involved in the state's #1 industry, tourism, but I was con-fident I could fit in the state's #2 industry, agriculture.

I wanted to develop my selling prowess in agronomy and needed to start by learning about the citrus business. Information was gen-erally available, and I had no problem committing to memory what I learned about the state's top crops like oranges, strawberries, toma-toes, and sod.

Also on my mind was making sure I brought my servant's heart with me to Florida—it had served me well in Montana, and I was sure it would serve me well once I landed a sales job in Florida. Bringing something more to my clients than just being a go-between was the way I had developed my sales career, and I expected I'd be able to do so going forward.

I began knocking on doors looking for a sales job and found a roadblock I did not completely anticipate. It was the Good Ol' Boys' Network. As I was not a Florida native and did not have a degree in agronomy, I had two strikes against me. I didn't speak "citrus-ese" or "degree-ese" or "Gator-ese," as so many of the University of Florida graduates did. I didn't wear the school's Kelly Blue & Orange as a way of identifying myself with the state's biggest university.

Frankly, I proudly presented myself as an outsider. Had I presented myself any other way, I would not have been true to the person I am, and I would have had a hard time trying to pull it off, even had I wanted to. But not being one of Florida's Good Ol' Boys placed a huge hurdle in front of me…and I took it as a challenge to be met head-on.

What I brought with me to Florida was a mindset that made me sure I could overcome the Good Ol' Boys' Network and succeed, chiefly by being the same salesman I was when I was in Montana. I took a job with a multinational crop nutrient company based in France, which was just starting to develop some new markets, Florida being one of them. Thanks to the research I had done when I was relocating and some of the learning I kept on doing, I landed a sales position with this company, and I was able to bring some revolutionary new technologies to citrus, sugar cane, vegetable, and sod growers all over my region.

Not being part of the Good Ol' Boys' Network, I would soon discover, turned out to be a significant asset as opposed to any kind of detriment.

From the outside, it probably looked like I was at a real disadvantage versus others in Florida agronomy sales. But the fact that I was in a new place geographically, selling a new product, and trying to attract a whole new clientele from scratch meant that I had to put forth effort similar to what was required of me in developing my sales territory with beef ranchers in Montana. That's because I relied on myself, and not any network of well-connected people, to build my business. I made a point to keep learning about Florida's agriculture,

Florida's soil, Florida's advantages and challenges, and how the products I had to sell could best be applied. By bringing this new and advanced thinking to the area, I was really able to become an asset for my customers' businesses.

In a Florida watermelon field, enjoying the "fruits" of my labor

I knew the Good Ol' Boys' Network was conducting business the way they always did—"Go talk to this guy, use my name, and he'll buy from you..."—while I was able to show why I was selling a superior product as well as the most progressive practices that their businesses could utilize. The result? In just 18 months my Florida region moved up to the company's top-20 sales areas for profit contribution! The company had more than 1,900 sales areas in 33 different countries around the world and I had been able to develop sales in an area where everyone knew everyone else in the business—except me.

Did I mention that all this happened between 2004 and 2005? The second Gulf War was underway, and the French government wasn't providing any help in that effort, a fact that didn't sit well with many Americans. More than once I had to deflect snide comments about my company's home country and turn my customers' attention to the benefits of employing my company's products.

My sales success probably had a lot to do with it, but I learned to love Florida. Hurricanes excepted, the weather is generally pleasant, and the sun shines pretty much every day. I would roam across my customers' sod farms during the middle of a beautiful day and marvel at how deep green the acres were all around me. The grass on these sod farms is like an iceberg in that we see a few inches of lush, green grass above-ground but not the deep roots that were key to the grass's health. I would check the strawberry patches, reach down, and pick a strawberry that was the biggest, ripest, and, therefore, sweetest one I could find. As I bit into the fruit, I would think about my friends back home in Montana and think: "If only they could see me now…"

I would drive into a customer's orange grove and not only be overcome by how delicious the smell of the fruit truly was, but also by the realization that this delicious scent was part of what I did for a living. That gave me a feeling of happiness that is hard to explain. I would realize that the fruit was so juicy and healthy in great part because of my work, which filled me with pride. Then I would meet with my customer and know that he had given me a chance in this business, in this state. My customer had listened to what I had to say about how I could help him with my products and expertise, and he had decided to buy from me instead of the Good Ol' Boys he'd known for years.

That knowledge made me feel grateful. So grateful.

It was while I was in Florida that I came to the full realization that I work to live; I don't live to work. Sure, I understood that while I trained working dogs and sold to ranches in Montana, but in Florida I embraced the mentality. I was doing work that I enjoyed, and that work was fueling a life that I enjoyed. Getting up in the morning to work didn't feel like drudgery at all; it was a joy to meet new people, see people I'd known for a while, and help people find answers to their questions. Viewing, tasting, and experiencing the results of my work—be they the juicy strawberries I could pick right off the plant or the long, flat meadow of dark green grass—was always fulfilling. The money I earned was, of course, absolutely appreciated.

But receiving a check was in no way the highlight of any workday.

Another thing that became readily apparent was how lucky I was to be in sales. In what other discipline can a person be a success in two places as completely different from one another as the mountains of western Montana and the flatlands of south Florida? Someone who spends his life in Florida may never see snow, while someone who spends his life in Montana may never see an ocean. The mining and ranching that takes place in Montana could never happen in Florida. The climate and the landscape are completely different. Many crops that grow in Florida could not rise from the ground in Montana, for instance. I knew that leaving Montana and arriving in Florida would take me out of sales to the world's best ranchers and put me into a business that would be completely different.

But being in the business of sales allowed me to move seamlessly from Montana to Florida. My professional life, I realized, does not depend on a whole lot more than my desire to help my customers. Of course, I have to learn and know as much as I can about the products I'm selling. I need to know how my products can help my customers and aid them in reaching their goals. I must be proficient in following up, making sure that deliveries are made to my customers on time and in the quantity and condition my customers expect. These are the basics of sales, whether it's sales of computer chips or potato chips.

Think about the challenges I overcame in Florida. Could those Good Ol' Boy salespeople pick up, move 2,000 miles away, and successfully sell to the ranchers I sold to in Montana? Probably not, at least not with the attitude that comes with being a part of the Good Ol' Boys' Network. People who rely on the Good Ol' Boys' Network for their livelihood are like the proverbial fish out of water if they're pulled from that group of people who spoon-feed them leads and sales. Those who are part of the Good Ol' Boys' Network don't draw on their own skills or their own desire to serve their clients; they develop the skills that allow them to serve the Network first and foremost, and that's what they do.

It's accurate to say that these people were not even in the business of sales. Rather, they were in the business of placeholding: A citrus grower needs fertilizer, a fertilizer company needs to get its product to citrus growers, members of the Good Ol' Boys' Network stick themselves in that place. They take the order, they deliver the product, they cash the checks…not because they're great salespeople and certainly not because they were serving their customers beyond getting the order delivered. They made these things happen only because they were in the right place as part of the Good Ol' Boys' Network.

Do members of the Good Ol' Boys' Network succeed? Do they ever move up? Sure, usually when a member of their network retires or moves on to another position within the network.

Think of the Good Ol' Boys' Network as the personification of a method, a strict selling method. Every meeting, every transaction happens only because someone follows a path that's been laid out before him. Just the way a selling method may dictate that someone follows

Step #1, then Step #2, then Step #3, the Good Ol' Boys' Network dictates that Salesman #1 went to school with the son of Sales Manager #2, which means Salesman #1 gets Account #3, and that's the way it is because that's the way the Good Ol' Boys' Network operates.

Although it may appear at first to be the Yellow Brick Road to riches, don't aspire to insert yourself into a network, especially if it's the Good Ol' Boys'; develop your own network and do it on your own terms. Bring a servant's heart to the relationship you have with your customers, feed that relationship, and good things will happen like your customers telling people about how great it is to work with you. That is when the calls come in and you start to develop your own network—based on merit, not just knowing the "right" people in the "right" places.

I'm not saying that there's anything wrong with inheriting an existing book of business in a new sales job. That sort of thing happens all the time. In fact, it would be unethical to ignore existing customers simply because they aren't customers you acquired yourself. Just don't rely on existing customers, or any existing network, for all your success.

Developing a network is like deriving income, in that developing a network is a by-product of bringing a servant's heart to each and every customer's needs. When you do that, you rely on the quiet confidence you bring to a relationship instead of relying on external "credentials," which you never really earn. When you develop your network, you'll present yourself as your customer's partner and play a part in your customer's success.

It really comes down to this: when you eschew the Good Ol' Boys' Network and develop a network of your own, you won't have to chase success because success will follow you.

CHAPTER 19

BE READY TO WALK AWAY

When you're a part of the Good Ol' Boys' Network, you owe your success to just about everyone but yourself. Someone connected you to a customer, the customer bought from you because you know someone else, everyone talks to everyone else in the network, everyone knows everyone's place in the network, everyone is satisfied with the way the network serves them, and everything stays that way. That's why you have to serve the Good Ol' Boys' Network first and foremost if you're a part of it.

This static business model gets in the way of you putting forth your best effort on behalf of your customer. How is that? Because if you're doing business as part of the Good Ol' Boys' Network, your job is largely to keep the network rolling as opposed to establishing a sales relationship in which you're truly serving your customer.

If there is (mentally) anyone else in the room when you and your customer meet, that means one or both of you is not giving 100% to the business relationship. In other words, one of you is serving someone else as well, be it a supplier or a contact or an in-law or a friend of a friend. A sales relationship that is not built on the bedrock principal that you are there to serve your customer—and your customer is there to reciprocate your commitment—will not last. It simply cannot flourish.

In my sales experience I have made it my purpose to work with the very best farmers and ranchers in the business, people who have been committed to producing the very best product they could possibly produce. I could have made the decision to simply build up a book of business as thick as possible, filled with as many milk producers as I could ably service in New Mexico and West Texas. I could have made a point to simply sell to every strawberry grower in Florida when I was there or everyone who owned an orange grove. But I made the decision to work with the very best because I wanted to be part of the reason why the best people in their field attain that status. Working with these people is, I have found, the best fit for me as a salesman and a person who brings a servant's heart to the task.

Hand in hand with that attitude is the knowledge that there are some people with whom I simply cannot work. I have begun negotiating terms with people and realized that the two of us were probably not going to be compatible. I've even seen a business relationship sour for me even when my customer didn't feel the same way.

In one case in particular, I didn't feel I was being respected. So I told my customer the name of a person I knew and suggested the reference may be a better fit for him.

In another case I just didn't feel like I was getting all the information I needed in order for my customer and me to both be successful. You know the type of person who gives you a little information at the introductory meeting, then a little more, or different information at the follow-up meeting, which causes you to have to retrace your steps. I call this sort of stunt The Shell Game, where someone keeps hiding and moving information in order to keep control of the situation. I had a new customer who did that during the first two meetings, and the little voice inside told me I should walk away. But I didn't. I came back for the third meeting, only to be presented with more new information, much of which contradicted what he'd told me earlier. At that point I told the guy that neither one of us was going to be successful if we didn't both share 100% of the relevant information with each other. He nodded his head aggressively, made a lot of blustery pronouncements about how he agreed with me and that we were going to have the greatest salesman/customer relationship of all time, and then he spent the next 90 minutes giving me what appeared to be loads of useful information, knowledge I could really employ in helping him feed his cows the right rations. I was excited as I got to work on the guy's behalf and was feeling good that I hadn't given up on the customer. A week later we were five minutes into our next meeting, and he was back to his old ways, playing The Shell Game with me. I gathered up my notes, extended my hand, suggested that we should not continue our relationship, wished him luck, and walked out the door.

I probably could have helped the guy's business if he'd been honest with me from the start. I definitely could have earned a beefy commission if I'd gotten that first sale with him, going completely through the process before drawing a conclusion about working with him. But I couldn't do that; I couldn't just make a sale to make a sale, and I couldn't comfortably sell to him without the knowledge that I had all the information to help his dairy produce at its maximum level.

Then there's the problem of late payments. A relationship with a customer can be a pleasure all the way through the process—smooth and apparently mutually beneficial—until the invoice you've presented goes unpaid. Chasing payment is one of the most awkward and time-consuming experiences ever for a sales professional. I have a friend who runs a tiny advertising agency in Denver, an agency that's burnished its reputation for getting jobs done quickly. A couple summers ago my friend performed some work for a tech company in

Kansas City and all went well until the tech company went 60 days without paying the invoice. After multiple emails and phone calls, my friend drove nine hours to Kansas City and met the tech company's CEO and CFO as they arrived at work. The tech company guys got defensive and said they were just trying to run a business—to which my friend cut in: "Hey, I run a business too. I've got employees, suppliers, and a landlord. I'm not here for me; I'm here for them." A moment later my friend left and told the two men to expect a phone call from his lawyer. The following morning, after a nine-hour drive back and far too much time on the phone with his lawyer, my friend found a FedEx envelope waiting for him at the office. Enclosed was a check from the tech company for the total amount on the invoice. The check cleared and my friend said that, while he was happy to finally get paid, he'd never get back the time he'd spent trying to secure that payment. It was time away from his family and it was time he could have been devoting to his other clients.

Once again: I don't work for money. And while payment means money changes hands, timely payment is more about how respect is built up in a healthy business relationship. Payment is the step in the sales process that completes the transaction and allows the two parties to feel positive about doing business together. A sales relationship that feels like the right fit can be completely spoiled by something as disrespectful as late payment. There's a very simple rule in business, which is something for you to always keep in mind: if someone agrees to buy something, he or she needs to pay for it.

The same goes for me, the salesman: I keep my word on something as big as a product delivery or something as small as a baseball cap bearing my company's logo. If I say I'm going to do something, I'm going to do it. My customers know that, and they treat me with the same respect when it comes to their side of the relationship, be it providing me with information or on-time payment.

Prompt payment is often one of the overlooked ingredients in making sure a customer is the right fit. If a customer doesn't pay the bill in a timely manner, and I am required to spend time collecting the money, that takes time away from servicing the customers who do pay their bills in a timely manner, and that's not fair to them. Always make payment terms clear to the customer on the front end of a transaction, and make sure they agree to those terms. Then, if payment is late, there is no room for debate, but just a dialogue on how the situation can be resolved now and going forward.

Whenever I've felt I was not the right fit for someone, I've been honest about it. I've never been surly, I've always shaken the person's hand, and I've always wished that person well, acknowledging that someone else would be the right fit.

In sales, it's all about being the right fit.

If you're in sales, your job is, of course, to make sales. "Sales" isn't just the title of your position; it's your one-word job description. You may find it antithetical to your professional purpose to even consider walking away from a sale. But you should always be prepared to walk away from a situation that doesn't feel right. It is the right decision on every level, and in the long run, it's the best decision for all involved.

Go for the right fit. The sale will happen. Success will follow. And you'll feel better for it.

CHAPTER 20

CAN I REALLY HELP YOUR SALES CAREER?

'm proud of the success I've had during my 30-plus years in sales. But I'm much prouder of the way I have achieved that success. Whether I'm looking at the image of myself in the mirror or the image of the Sangre de Cristo Mountains standing proudly outside my office window, I'm doing so with the comfort that I have earned the reputation I have in sales through honesty, authenticity, and hard work.

These attributes may seem lost in today's fast-paced cyber world, relics of a forgotten era. But the fact is that sales is a business that dates back hundreds of years and has always involved the interaction of two parties—that is, two people. You do not sell to a machine. You do not sell to an association. You do not sell to a corporation. You sell to the person sitting before the keyboard of that machine, you sell to the person representing the association, you sell to the person tasked with acquiring what you're selling for a corporation. Keep that in mind when you consider that 92% of all interactions that a salesperson has with a customer happen over the phone.[7] When you're on the phone, you're not talking to a machine, an association, or a corporation. You're talking to another person.

People have always admired honesty, authenticity, and hard work, and I'm very confident that people always will. Put these qualities on display every time you interact with your customers, and you will be seen as a guide and a partner in the buying journey.

You will be a person who is "of service."

I have been successful because I have been of service to people. I have been rigorously honest and authentic in my working relationships and believe I have developed those relationships based on these qualities. I have worked hard on behalf of all my business partners and, finally, I believe I have had success in my career because I am a singularly unique individual...

AND SO ARE YOU!

I believe I can help you become better and more proficient in sales by helping you understand the importance of bringing the things that make you unique to your job. You can be honest and authentic, just like I am. You can work just as hard as I have. But displaying these qualities in common with me would not make you a clone of me; it would simply make you the best *YOU* can be as a salesperson.

Being the best YOU can be is the way for you to achieve mastery in the business of sales, because someone with mastery knows he has something special to offer: his own matchless self! A person who's achieved mastery knows she will get more back from the sales relationship than she ever puts in—and that's saying something since a person who's achieved mastery puts 100% into everything.

A person who's achieved mastery doesn't go out looking for acceptance...Good Ol' Boys' Network, anyone? No, a person who's achieved mastery looks for a need to fill and fills it.

> **"Your need for acceptance can make you invisible in this world."** —*Jim Carrey*

By directing my energy toward my customers and filling their needs, I have enjoyed more personal fulfillment as well as financial success. Long ago I realized that these two things follow each other in that order. Money doesn't bring fulfillment or happiness, but if you go after the kind of fulfillment that comes with helping another person, you will find financial success.

Today my job is to be around wonderful, incredible animals, making sure they're as healthy as I can help them be. It never gets old to me to put on my big rubber boots and step into the pen at one of my client's dairy farms. One or two of the cows are always a little playful, stepping up to me and letting me tap them on the head like they're dogs. "Hello Sweetheart," I often say to a cow who is displaying social skills.

> **"An honest man's pillow is his peace of mind."**
> **—John Mellencamp**

Knowing that I'm helping these cows stay healthy is always a source of great fulfillment to me. Knowing that I helped people whose business it is to draw a living from those cows doubles the fulfillment.

When I reflect on my sales career, it's this kind of realization that truly inspires me and makes me grateful that I long ago learned that the key to a great sales career is developing and maintaining a mutually beneficial relationship with each customer.

That's what I hope you get out of this book. Your master is not your sales, your commission, or your network. Your master is your customer. You serve him; he serves you. The benefits for you both flow from that. Even more, your masters are your values, your motives, and your conscience.

CHAPTER 21

STILL...I HAVE A LOT TO LEARN

Leaders in a variety of industries and the military often refer to "known knowns," "known unknowns," and "unknown unknowns." Basically, what these three things represent are obstacles that a person knows exists and knows how to overcome, obstacles that a person knows exists and doesn't know much about how to overcome, and obstacles that a person doesn't even know exist...so how can that person overcome them?

Scientific research is often based on investigating known unknowns by way of developing a hypothesis and then testing it.[8] The result of the test, of course, reveals new knowledge, and knowledge is a powerful tool in any endeavor.

The point is that more than three decades in the sales business has allowed me to gather up a lot of "known knowns." But I also know that I don't know everything there is to know about selling. I don't know everything there is to know about dairy nutrition. I know that I have to be ready for the "known unknowns" and the "unknown unknowns" that will inevitably show up as I perform my job. That preparation starts with my being humble enough to know that these things are out there and that I have to learn how best to overcome them.

Dairy nutrition, for instance, is constantly changing. It's probably more accurate to say that it's forever evolving. There are always new products and new combinations to learn about and there are scores of reasons why the ration that's right for one dairy producer's cows is completely wrong for another producer's cows. Keeping on top of everything related to the subject allows me to continue improving in my work. But I know there's always a chance that some piece of knowledge will get past me.

The point is that I need to keep learning. Once I learn something, I know it, and once I know something, I can learn more about it. Basically, learning leads to knowledge, knowledge leads to understanding, understanding leads to the desire to learn more.

There are two specific types of knowledge for people in every culture and profession. General knowledge is common, widely known, and pretty much indisputable. The sky is blue. 2 + 2 = 4. Water is wet. Each of these statements is based in fact. Knowing these things will not get you very far in sales or any other endeavor.

Then there's specialized knowledge, which is acquired only by really drilling down on a subject. Scientists are a font of specialized knowledge…in their fields. I know a mathematician who's got an I.Q. well over 200, but he has trouble spelling the word "cat." If you think that sounds absurd, consider that Albert Einstein failed his entrance exam for Swiss Federal Polytechnic. His physics and math scores on the test were exceptional, but his marks on the other subjects were so poor they tanked the whole test.[9] My own specialized knowledge covers a variety of subjects from goats to dairy cows to motorcycles to mountain ranges, but when a customer asked me what he should see and do during an upcoming trip to New Orleans, I told my customer I'd get back to him.

The fact is that I've never been to New Orleans. But I know someone who knows the city well. I sent a message to that person, a longtime friend who'd gone to school there, and was able to deliver a bevy of great tourist information to my client a day later.

> "Everyone is ignorant. Only on different subjects."
> —*Will Rogers*

General knowledge is fairly easy to acquire, while specialized knowledge can take years of research and hard work to become part of your knowledge base. Specialized knowledge falls under the headings of "known unknowns" and "unknown unknowns." I, for instance, don't know anything about a complex financial instrument like a collateralized debt obligation. But if I needed to learn about it, I know exactly whom I would call in order to start my education.

And that's the point. While you will be rewarded for always learning more and knowing more, you need to be astute and agile enough to know where you can get information if you need it. Knowledge is everywhere in this world, and it's just waiting for you to discover it!

About 100 years ago, the legendary automobile manufacturer Henry Ford took a Chicago newspaper to court. The reason was that the paper had run several editorials in which, among other statements, Ford was called "an ignorant pacifist" for pushing to keep the United States out of World War I.

When the suit was tried, the newspaper's attorneys put Mr. Ford on the stand for the purpose of putting his ignorance on display. They asked him a series of questions, most of them very pointed and requiring knowledge of extreme minutiae. One question was whether Mr. Ford knew how many soldiers the British sent to the Colonies to quash the Revolution in 1776. Ford's reply? "I do not know the exact number of soldiers the British sent over, but I have heard that it was a considerably larger number than ever went back."[10] The questions continued, and Mr. Ford had finally had enough. He pointed his finger at the lawyer who had asked a particularly offensive question, he looked the man in the eye, and he said: "If I should really WANT to answer the foolish question you have just asked, or any of the other questions you have been asking me, let me remind you that I have a row of electric push-buttons on my desk, and by pushing the right button, I can summon to my aid men who can answer ANY question I desire to ask concerning the business to which I am devoting most of my efforts. Now, will you kindly tell me WHY I should clutter up my mind with general knowledge, for the purpose of being able to answer questions, when I have men around me who can supply any knowledge I require?"[11]

Pretty good logic, isn't it? Certainly not the kind of logic that would come from an ignorant man.

This story about Henry Ford is the perfect illustration of two important points in sales or pretty much every other business. The first point is that, no matter how much you know, there is always more to learn. Second, the best way to gain that knowledge is to ask questions of people who are well-versed in a particular subject. Asking questions always yields new information and never makes you look dumb or ignorant. Furthermore, it really isn't bothersome to another person—many people are flattered when they're asked a question. Finally, asking questions does not only satisfy curiosity; it also leads to more curiosity and a desire to learn more.

> "Curiouser and curiouser!"
>
> *—Alice from Lewis Carroll's*
> **Alice's Adventures in Wonderland**

The smartest people in business know they don't have all the answers, but they do ask a lot of questions.[12] Take a tip from them.

You don't need a personal assistant.

You don't need a staff.

You don't even need "a row of electronic push-buttons" on your desk.

You simply have to show your customer that you're willing and able to get the information he or she is looking for and then go about the process of doing so.

Your customer will always appreciate that you didn't rush to answer a question you weren't 100% sure you could answer. He will greatly appreciate that you took the time, and made the extra effort, to secure the proper information.

When you show extra effort on behalf of the relationship that you're never done building with your customer, you are showing that you're "of service." You're showing that you set a high bar for yourself, and you're bringing your customer a higher level of knowledge.

In short, you're feeding the relationship.

CONCLUSION

I believe in what I sell. I am proud of what I sell. I always have felt that way. I couldn't put into the job what it takes to sell if I didn't believe that I was offering my customers the best products and information I could offer.

I am never "off-loading" anything. I don't "dump" product. What I'm selling is neither my problem nor my burden. As for the considerable amount of time I put into my sales, driving all over New Mexico and West Texas, meeting with the wonderful dairy producers who I'm honored to have as clients, I will never get that time back. So I'd better make the best of it.

Believing in and being proud of what you sell are keys to authenticity. If you believe what you're selling is the best product of its kind, you will enthusiastically recommend it and your authenticity will shine through. You will confidently and humbly become the spokesperson that the product truly deserves.

When you believe in what you sell, you don't have to put on airs or embellish anything you're saying; you can simply cater to your customer's needs and guide him through the buying process. By putting everything you have into the relationship you have with the customer—and always being willing to give more—you will show by all your words and actions that you are putting the customer first.

Speaking of giving, I always tell people in sales that they should give freely and abundantly. Consider the 18 months I gave to Ben and

Justine, working on their dairy entirely without recompense. The time I gave certainly paid off professionally and personally as these people have become dear friends. I gave my time, and I gave plenty of product samples…you should too.

A friend reminded me once of the Grateful Dead, the legendary rock band that inspired a worldwide following called Deadheads during their 30 years together. The band started in San Francisco in 1965, and one of the things that made them unique was that they'd set up a stage in a park somewhere, usually in their hometown's Golden Gate Park, and start playing. People would show up and—VOILA!—everyone enjoyed a free concert. The Dead also had no problem with fans recording their shows and duplicating their bootleg tapes. While every other rock band in the world considers such action criminal, the Dead encouraged it as these bootlegs allowed more and more people to experience their concerts. By the time the band's leader Jerry Garcia died in 1995, the band had sold 35 million albums, performed before crowds of more than 100,000 (paying) fans, and amassed a fortune so vast that each member had a personal worth in the tens of millions. "Making a sale" was never the band's priority; making music and developing a bond with their fans was.

In sales and in your personal life, give first. That's the essence of the servant's heart. Your customers, your friends, and your loved ones will recognize that quality in you and reciprocate. Give first. You will never regret it.

Which brings me my final point…

Have fun.

In my own life, I insist on it. My saying is, "If there ain't some fun in the deal, deal me out!" Sales is a fun business, and if you're having fun, you'll bring a positive energy to everything you do. Sales is not a grind. It's not a race. It's not about moving product or meeting quotas.

Sales is about meeting people, interacting with people, and helping people.

Sales is about being "of service."

NOTES

PART 1
1. https://www.resourcefulselling.com/closing-the-sale-statistics/
2. https://blog.thebrevetgroup.com/21-mind-blowing-sales-stats
3. Ibid

PART 2
1. https://goatwiththeflow.wordpress.com/about/
2. https://www.outtherecolorado.com/a-goat-could-be-your-best-packing-partner/
3. https://www.cnbc.com/2018/11/20/us-workers-to-forfeit-half-their-vacation-time-this-year.html
4. https://www.goalcast.com/2017/05/11/thomas-edison-quotes-motivate-never-quit/
5. https://www.goalcast.com/2017/05/11/thomas-edison-quotes-motivate-never-quit/
6. https://markets.businessinsider.com/news/stocks/florida-economy-facts-2019-5-1028214563#there-are-actually-scammers-in-florida-who-try-to-sell-people-swampland3
7. https://blog.thebrevetgroup.com/21-mind-blowing-sales-stats
8. https://academic.oup.com/jxb/article/60/3/712/453685
9. https://allthatsinteresting.com/albert-einstein-facts#3
10. https://medium.com/@issacqureshi/what-is-specialized-knowledge-here-is-a-quote-from-henry-ford-that-may-explain-d469292edd13
11. Ibid.
12. https://www.fastcompany.com/3056318/how-the-most-successful-people-ask-questions

ABOUT THE AUTHOR

Clancy Clark intends to change the sales industry with his message. That's a lofty goal, but it's one that Clancy thinks is completely within his reach. The way he intends to do that is to inspire others in the business to place helping people as the top priority in the sales equation. Only when sales professionals make helping people the most important standard in the industry will the historically negative stereotypes of salespeople finally fade away.

"Life is an adventure," declares Clancy. "The way I've lived my life, I believe, demonstrates that belief." Born in Arkansas and raised in Colorado, he lived 20 years in Montana, four years back in Arkansas, two years in Texas, six years in Florida, eight years in New Mexico, and resides today on a spectacular property surrounded by southern Colorado's Sangre de Cristo Mountains. When not working with his clients—Clancy is hiking with friends and his loyal goats, literally blazing new trails in his charity work, or traveling the country in his adventure RV. He basks in the company of his friends, his family, and the natural world he loves so much.

Throughout his adult life, Clancy has pursued personal development, self-actualization, and spiritual growth. He realized early on that life is not a race to be won, but a daily pursuit of personal fulfillment that can only be attained by placing service to others as the imperative value. He brings this understanding to his work and has applied it to his sales career for more than 30 years, a career that has seen him achieve results so remarkable that his numbers speak for themselves.

Ironically, Clancy didn't always see himself as a salesman. In fact, it was when he was a young man, working as a sheepherder, that he took a career aptitude test with an eye on what might be next for himself. The results indicated that Clancy would make a very capable salesman, news that Clancy took as a distinct negative. When he looked in the mirror, the last thing he wanted to see was a salesman! Nevertheless, Clancy has evolved to be sincerely proud of his role in sales, serving his customers with the same passion he exudes in all areas of his life.

"The beautiful irony," says Clancy, "Is that by placing service to others above material success, more sales, money, and recognition actually do flow toward a salesperson, more than a salesperson could realize by just chasing sales for the sake of selling. By embracing the values and concepts I write about in 'Selling By Serving,' I have enjoyed abundance in every area of my life. Sales is an honorable profession, if one chooses to make it so."

What makes Clancy so authentic and qualified to write this book is that he has actually done everything he suggests to the reader. He has lived it for more than three decades with amazing results and, more importantly, he has been happy and fulfilled in both his work and his personal life. "To me, being happy is the greatest thing a person can achieve," Clancy states. "One of my favorite things is helping others become happier. It adds to my own happiness immensely. I happen to know a lot about what I consider true success in sales, so, it's one area where I can make a difference. That's what 'Selling By Serving' is all about."